The Photography of

John Muir Wood 1805–1892

An Accomplished Amateur

Sara Stevenson · Julie Lawson · Michael Gray

Scottish National Portrait Gallery

Dirk Nishen Publishing

front cover

Citadel of Namur from a bridge over the Sambre
gold toned uranium print from a calotype negative
'W'
paper, 'J WHA[TMAN] TURKEY [MILL] 184[ ]'
120 × 151 mm
PGP-W76

back cover

Citadel of Namur from a bridge over the Sambre
7 August 1847
calotype negative
125 x 154 mm
PGP-W77

This book is dedicated to Sir Alan Muir Wood and Paul Muir Wood
whose generous gift to the Scottish nation has made it possible

Design: Michael Gray
Photography: Ian Jones, London
Typesetting: PCS Typesetting, Frome
Lithographic origination: ORT Kirchner + Graser, D-Berlin
Printing: H Heeneman, D-Berlin
Binding: Lüderitz & Bauer, D-Berlin

The publisher wishes to thank all of the parties involved

ISBN 1 85378 007 3

Acknowledgements

We are indebted to our colleagues for their help in the preparation of this book.

In particular we should like to thank the following people who have been most generous in their assistance: Paul Muir Wood; Brian Coe; John Cranmer; Roy Flukinger; Barbara Gray; Murray Johnston; Alison Morrison-Low; Pamela Roberts; David Williams and Larry Schaaf, Carolyn Bloore, Ruari McLean, Roy Fluckinger and Sheena MacDougall for their generous help with the Cundall/Cundell family. We are especially grateful to Sheila Smith for the meticulous typescript.

NOTES

The details of John Muir Wood's biography were researched by Paul Muir Wood and we are grateful to him for so generously sharing his knowledge with us. Quotations from the family correspondence and Wood's diary refer to documents in the collection of Paul Muir Wood.

John Muir Wood: The Man and the Photographer
By Sara Stevenson and Julie Lawson

Life and Music

John Muir Wood was not a professional photographer, but a musician. He was born in 1805, into an Edinburgh family of piano-makers and music publishers.[1] A pianist, teacher, musicologist and impressario, Wood used his camera to record his times, his travels and his friends. But more than that, his photography, particularly his landscape photography, was informed by the same aesthetic purposes that guided his musical and intellectual life.

European sophistication was an asset in the music business, and John Muir Wood was sent abroad to acquire it in 1826. He first went to Paris where he was accepted as a pupil by one of the most celebrated pianoforte teachers of the day, Johann Peter Pixis.[2] Evidently, he was an able student. Pixis esteemed him well enough to reduce his usual teaching rate in order that Wood's financial distress — the family business was in some difficulty at the time and his funding was not always sufficient for his needs — should not hinder his education. Pixis also introduced him to musical society, so that Wood not only developed considerable skill as a pianist, but also gained invaluable knowledge of contemporary music and performance. His taste then and later, though broad, was most enthusiastically for the great Romantic composers, particularly Beethoven, Mendelssohn and Weber.

As well as with a cultural breadth, Wood's experience in Paris endowed him with an urbanity that gives a special quality to his writing. He could be laconic, and he could be witty. He sent back to Scotland reports of musical performances that he attended. Among them is this critical account of a Rossini opera, *The Siege of Corinth*, written in 1827:

> ... there are not above 3 or 4 pretty airs in the whole piece, the rest is made up of recitative & stuff that has no meaning in it; from time to time we were regaled with bursts of noise, to inspire the actors no doubt with a proper vigour & let them know when to throw about their arms lay their hands on their swords, daggers &[c]; then some love sick damsel comes in to calm the fury of the disputants ... as too long a continuation of this might have the effect of a lullaby on the audience, the triangles are called in to dissipate any propensity that the public may have in this way, thus they go on act after act till at last down come half a dozen temples with a tremendous crash, the policy of this cannot be too much admired for it rouses most effectually all those who may not have been able to resist the embraces of Morpheus, & gives them back the powers of speech in time to descant on the excellency of the piece, & to declare, how this was *charmant*, that *magnifique*, & t'other *delicieux*.

Despite their financial difficulties, the firm decided that Wood should take further lessons in Vienna in 1827. His father, who took a liberal, eighteenth-century attitude towards spelling, wrote: 'Except you appear as a Star of the first magnitude we will feel great disappointment, as high expectations is formed of you here — the professional people are all dubling their diligence and some of them are getting into sober habits least you ecclips them, at all events we think you ought to studee under a Master of higher celebrity ... Since it has been known that you are under Pixis tutian it has been wisperd about that he is only a Secendary teacher.' Wood's father wanted him to study under Johann Nepomuk Hummel, but in the event he became the pupil of Carl

1 John Muir Wood's father, Andrew Wood (1765-1829), entered into partnership with John Muir in 1797 and, on Muir's death in 1818, entered a second partnership with George Small. The firm manufactured square pianos, organs, harps and drums and published sheet music.

2 Johann Peter Pixis (1788-1874) piano teacher and composer.

3 Johann Nepomuk Hummel (1778-1837) and Carl Czerny (1791-1857).

Czerny,[3] who was himself the pupil of Beethoven and had taught Liszt some ten years earlier. He was able to reassure his father, 'as for studies, one cannot come to a better place than Germany, for the natives are famous for their perseverance and I can assure you I have learned as much since I came here as all the time I was in Paris: I will not say that one can find politeness or that witty and pleasing manner that the French have of speaking on every subject; but whatever a German knows, he in general knows well.' Wood's acquaintance in Vienna 'lies principally among the Poles who are in general very clever and know several languages ... They almost all play some instrument, and are well acquainted with the theory of music.'

Both in Paris and in Vienna, Wood was able to advance a more general education. He achieved an excellent command of four languages and, in a letter of June 1827, he hinted at his interest in science which was later to prove essential in the practice of photography: 'I went to the University to hear a lecture on Optics, & although from my confined knowledge of the language I understood but a small portion of it, still it did not fail to interest me; when it was finished the Professor showed me his collection of Instruments, pointed out their different uses, and even performed experiments on some of them that I might better understand what he meant.'

Letters to his friend, Thomas May, clearly revealed a juvenile romantic vein that does not appear in his letters home. Thomas May's response to one of these in 1826 relates the course of his own fickle love life: 'if I can call to aid a slight portion of your effrontery, and keep a respectable footing with a Lass, who after reading the flaming Account of your delicious morsel I ought perhaps to be silent upon, I shall consider myself a happy fellow ... she is in my eye lovely not only in figure, face ... but disposition, in short, to use your words, made for Love.'

John Muir Wood returned to Edinburgh in 1828, 'a remarkably good pianist',[4] and set up as a music teacher. In 1829, his father died and he joined his brother George (plate 2) in the family business which was then in a state of confusion. In rebuilding the business, they faced 'a task requiring time, temper, and untiring energy and tact',[5] which they achieved in combining George's business acumen and John's expert knowledge of music. John Muir Wood's particular achievement, both in association with his brother and after he had moved to Glasgow in 1848, was the advancement of music through the organisation of concerts and his research into the history of Scottish music. He arranged concerts for celebrated musicians including Chopin, Liszt and Charles Hallé. Wood also researched and published articles on music, including the entry on Scottish music in George Grove's *Dictionary of Music and Musicians*, and a serious and influential edition of *The Songs of Scotland*.[6]

In 1851, at the age of 45, Wood married the young Helen Kemlo Stephen (plates 3 and 4) who bore him no less than thirteen children. He died after a long life in his house at Cove on the west coast of Scotland in 1892. 'His habits were quiet,' said one obituary, 'and his life was void of exciting incident.'[7] This 'most modest of men'[8] left one unexpected legacy which is the subject of this book: nine hundred photographs and negatives taken mostly in the 1840s and 1850s in the experimental years of the art.

The survival of what may be John Muir Wood's complete output is in itself remarkable and gives us an invaluable insight into the practice of photography in its infancy. His work is varied and inventive in technique and far-ranging in subject

4 Biography of John Muir Wood in *The Dictionary of National Biography*.

5 Biography of George Wood in *The Biographical Magazine*, October 1887, p 147.

6 *The Songs of Scotland*, illustrated with historical, biographical, and critical notices by George Farquhar Graham, published by J Muir Wood and Co, Glasgow and Edinburgh, 1848 and 1849 in two volumes. Revised edition published as *The Popular Songs and Melodies of Scotland*, 1884.

7 Obituary in *The Musical Herald*, 1 August 1892.

8 Herbert Kemlo Wood, writing of his father's appearing as an accompanist during the interval of the Chopin concert in 1848. 'Mme. Adelasio de Marguerittes gave him [Chopin] a rest while she sang three times in romantic Italian airs. She was accompanied by my father, most modest of men, who refused to let his name appear on the programme and would not accept a fee.' *The Glasgow Bulletin*, 27 September 1848.

matter. His photographs include portraits and figure compositions; studies of sculpture, paintings and architecture; townscape, and, most importantly, landscape. But the interest of these photographs is not merely academic. They are the work of a man capable of originality in the science of photography as well as in the art of photography — a rare combination.

Friends and Associates

How Wood first became interested in photography is not known and his photographic associates are only sporadically documented. Any attempt to map his sources of information and the people who influenced him can only be a partial explanation of the background to his photography. His capacity for self-education can be seen not only in his letters home in his student days but also in the photographs themselves. Wood travelled extensively in Europe so he could have met and talked to photographers anywhere between Ireland and Austria, or seen their work in the exhibitions which were already becoming common in the early 1850s. He could also have understood articles on photography in at least four foreign languages. It would clearly be a mistake to regard his knowledge of photography as confined to Edinburgh and Glasgow especially as he apparently did not join photographic societies in either city.

In the early years, photography was an exciting, sociable affair. Enthusiasts exchanged prints, negatives and information. Wood's collection, as it now stands, includes work by at least two, and probably more, of the 1840s photographers — those named being Hugh Owen of Bristol[9] (fig 1) and Joseph Cundell[10](fig 2). Wood's association with the Cundell family is particularly interesting. They appear in several of his group photographs. James Nasmyth, the engineer, who knew three of the 'kind, gentle and genial' Cundell brothers in London, noted their combined knowledge of the sciences and arts: 'The elder brother was an admirable performer on the violoncello and he treated us ... with noble music from Beethoven and Mozart. My special friend George ... was thoroughly versed in general science and was moreover a keen politician. He had a most happy faculty of treating complex subjects, both in science and politics, in a thoroughly common sense manner. His two brothers had a fine feeling for art and, indeed, possessed no small skill as practical artists.'[11]

The most notable of these brothers, in photographic terms, was George Smith Cundell (1798-1882), the agent for Patrick Maxwell Stuart's West Indian estates and the author of a practical and genuinely useful treatise on the calotype process. Three of his brothers appear in Wood's photographs: Charles Edward Cundell (1805-1880), who probably worked for the London and Westminster Bank and was also a painter (fig 5); Joseph Cundell (born 1802), an agent for the British Linen Bank, and Henry Cundell (1810-1886), a landscape painter (plate 45). The family came originally from Leith, the port to the north of Edinburgh, but three of the four moved down to London. About twenty photographs in Wood's collection seem likely to have been taken by one or other of the Cundells. Curiously, the identified photographs of London subjects are not by George or Henry, who are both known to have taken photographs, but by Joseph Cundell, who stayed in Leith: presumably he spent some time with his brothers in London.

The association with Hugh Owen suggests that Wood had a connection,

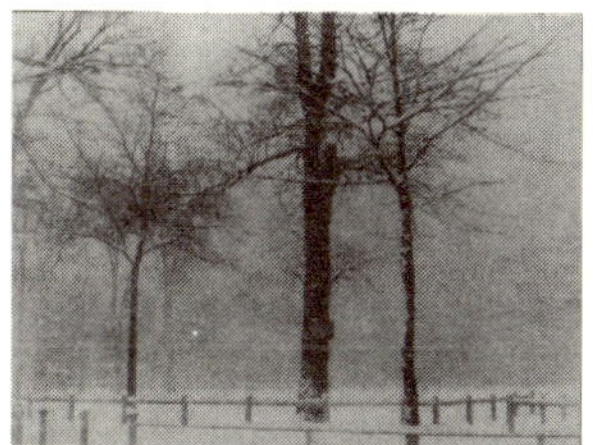

Fig 1 Hugh Owen
Queen Square, Bristol, about 1847
salt print from a calotype negative
Scottish National Portrait Gallery

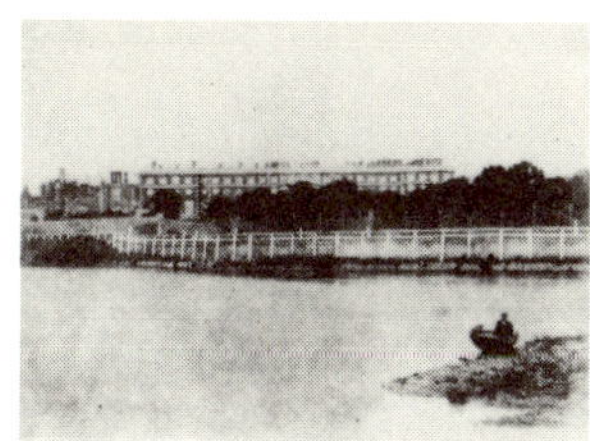

Fig 2 Joseph Cundell
Hampton Court across the Thames, about 1847
copper/tin-toned salt paper print from a calotype negative
Scottish National Portrait Gallery

9 Hugh Owen (1808-1897) of Bristol, Fellow of the Society of Antiquaries, Chief Cashier of the Great Western Railway, amateur photographer working with the calotype process. The wrapper in which Hugh Owen's photographs were sent to Wood is inscribed, 'Kindly obliged by Jh.[*or* H] Cundall Es^r Sey. C.C.'

10 Confusingly, this is not the same man as Joseph Cundall (1818-1875), publisher and, later, a professional photographer in partnership with P H Delamotte, Robert Howlett and Downes. The calotypes are identified as the work of 'Jh. Cundell' in the album belonging to James Eckford Lauder (now in the Edinburgh Central Library), which contains some of Wood's photographs, and identifies the portraits of 'Joseph Cundell', 'C Cundell' and 'Henry and Lucy Cundell'.
Information on the Cundell family comes from correspondence with the late L S Cundell in the Edinburgh Central Library.

11 *James Nasmyth, Engineer. An Autobiography*, ed. Samuel Smiles, London, 1891, p149.

informal or formal, with the London Calotype Club, to which Owen belonged. The Calotype Club, formed in 1847, was an amateur association of twelve members who met to discuss photography in each other's houses, and was composed of some of the liveliest intelligences of the day. They were concerned with the science and the aesthetics of the art, and as a group had the necessary knowledge to reinforce their practical skill.

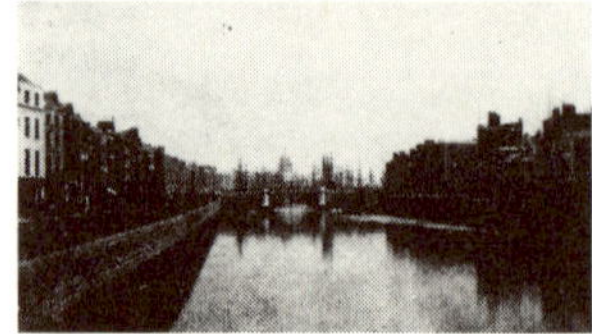

Fig 3 John Muir Wood
Dublin, the River Liffey
carbon print from a calotype negative
Scottish National Portrait Gallery

One society that Wood is known to have joined was the Glasgow Philosophical Society.[12] His association with this scientific body brought him into contact with several notable chemists, particularly Walter Crum,[13] who was Vice-President of the Society when Wood became a member in 1850. Walter Crum was a calico printer who was interested in photographic chemistry and who was praised in *The Journal of the Photographic Society* for being 'as remarkable for his knowledge of chemical science as for his ingenuity and success in applying it to practice'.[14] Wood's interest in achieving a range of chemical colour, and his experiments in permanent printing seen in his carbon work, may well have been related to Crum's research.

From the physical evidence of the photographs themselves, Wood was likely to have known Charles John Burnett (1820-1907). Burnett, who lived in Edinburgh in the 1850s, was a founder member of the Photographic Society of Scotland in 1856 and was a vigorous experimenter searching for more stable substances for photography than silver. His most interesting and useful discoveries related to the carbon, platinum and uranium processes, two of which were practised by Wood in their early experimental stages.

Wood's knowledge of the science of photography is also likely to have come in part from his friendship with Dr Jasper MacAldin, an eye surgeon working in Belfast.[15] Wood photographed MacAldin demonstrating an electrical experiment with a 'thunder house' (plate 9), a parlour experiment in which a charge of electricity was sent through a little house which promptly fell down, (whether the skull in the photograph was also electrically wired or was merely there as a symbol of mortality, is not clear). MacAldin had lectured on electricity and also on chemistry and light. With his knowledge of optics linked to chemistry, there can be no doubt that he would have discussed photography with Wood. The group of photographs which Wood took in Ireland (fig 3) were probably taken during a visit to the MacAldin family who were long-standing friends of the Woods.

In Edinburgh in the mid 1840s, the obvious model for any photographer would have been the work of the partnership of David Octavius Hill and Robert Adamson. Their studio was in operation from 1843 to 1847 and they set the standard of technical and artistic excellence (see figs 4, 6 and 15). D O Hill, who was a landscape painter and Secretary of the Royal Scottish Academy, had much in common with John Muir Wood. One review of Hill's painting, in 1846, compared it with his singing of old Scots songs: 'His works always exhibit something of the highest beauty, — often a sort of tenderness as unexpected and as plaintive as the "owercome" of an old border ditty sung by himself.'[16] Hill drew his daughter, in 1852, sitting at the piano playing Beethoven,[17] so his household was familiar with the same music that formed Wood's taste. Wood even fulfilled one of Hill's ambitions by photographing Nuremberg.[18]

Wood was most directly associated with the art world through his

12 A certificate of Wood's membership is in Paul Muir Wood's collection.

13 Biography of Walter Crum in *Memoirs and Portraits of One Hundred Glasgow Men*, Glasgow, 1886, pp93-6.

14 George Wilson 'Some Actinic Phenomena relating to Photography', *The Journal of the Photographic Society* [later *The British Journal of Photography*], 23 May 1859, p 292.

15 *The Medical Register*, London. The 1855-1877 volumes have entries on James Jasper MacAldin.

16 Dr John Brown, review of the Royal Scottish Academy exhibition, *The Witness*, 22 April 1846.

17 Drawing by Hill now missing, known from a glass negative taken by Alexander Inglis in the Glasgow University Library.

18 'I have also an Idea that I would like to do Nuremberg [?] a work by itself. I have heard much of that ancient place and we have little of it yet in art.' Letter from D O Hill to David Roberts, 12 March 1845, ms in a private collection, quoted in full in John Ward and Sara Stevenson, *Printed Light*, Edinburgh, 1986, pp 36-38.

19 James Eckford Lauder and his brother, Robert Scott Lauder, were both members of the Photographic Society of Scotland from 1856.

20 Peter Graham, quoted in Lindsay Errington, *Master Class: Robert Scott Lauder and his pupils*, Edinburgh, 1983, p 32.

friendship with James Eckford Lauder (1811-1869) (fig 5), a genre, history and landscape painter and a member of the Royal Scottish Academy.[19] Wood's diary recorded in a characteristically laconic manner a tour of the west of Scotland with Lauder in 1841: 'Walked to Barone Cottage — which we took after seeing the fine view of Arran from the hill — no lack of water on the island — J E L took a sketch from the inn — a good sample of the dismal, for the day wet & gloomy — took up our abode in the eveng. — 25/- a week service & coals included.'

James Eckford Lauder owned an album of Wood's photographs which included ten groups. Despite the reference to landscape sketching in 1841, Lauder was, in the 1840s, substantially a genre and history painter, exhibiting pictures with titles like 'What shall I say?', 'Modesty and Vanity' or 'The Ballad'. There is one striking coincidence in subject between the photographs and Lauder's painting, in the picture he exhibited in 1854 called 'The Wishing Bone': the same idea as Wood's 'Mr Purdie and friends' (plate 43).

The photographic groups (plates 37 and 38) may well all have been taken in Leith, where Lauder's family and the Cundells lived, and as such are closely linked to an art circle. Of the people who are identified in the groups, Lauder and Charles and Henry Cundell were painters.

Constructing a photographic group was particularly difficult. The exposure times could be short, just a second or two. The greyhound standing by one of the groups (plate 38) is evidence of a fast lens. But the satisfactory arrangement of a group took long minutes rather than seconds, and required the first people placed in position to stay still while the other figures were posed and adjusted. If the individuals touched or supported one another, the risk of them moving was far greater. D O Hill used mechanical supports (which Wood did not) but, more importantly, employed remarkable skill in the arrangement of groups in which the figures linked and propped each other in an apparently natural manner (fig 6). He was helped in this by his artist friends who were both used to being exploited as models and interested in art experiment. In the Leith circle, Wood apparently found a similar amiable co-operation.

Wood's closely-constructed groups, such as fig 7, are not unlike Hill and Adamson's work. The looser compositions, such as plates 43 and 44, have a sculptural, frieze-like appearance which is similar to Lauder's painting of 'The Parable of the Ten Virgins' (fig 8). The figures are independent and relate to each other at a physical distance. The oddly sculptural effect of these photographs may well be a direct reflection of Lauder's influence, and has a parallel with the teaching practice of his brother, Robert Scott Lauder, who was Director of the Trustees Academy in Edinburgh from 1852. Lauder taught his students to draw from classical casts in the Academy, but not in the conventional way. He mounted the sculpture on castors and moved them into groups. They were lit from windows in the roof, and one student recalled the extraordinarily interesting result: 'I shall never forget the exquisite beauty of the middle tint or overshadowing which the statues had that were placed between the windows; those which were immediately underneath them were of course in a blaze of light, and we had all gradations of light, middle tint and shadow.'[20] It should be remembered that the calotype process which Wood, like Hill and Adamson, used was much admired by the painters for its ability to catch the subtle gradations of light.

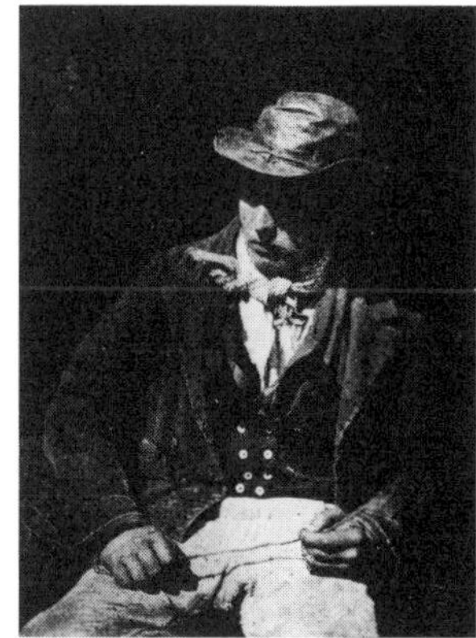

Fig 4 D O Hill and Robert Adamson
Willie Liston, Newhaven fisherman, 1843-1846
salt print from a calotype negative
Scottish National Portrait Gallery

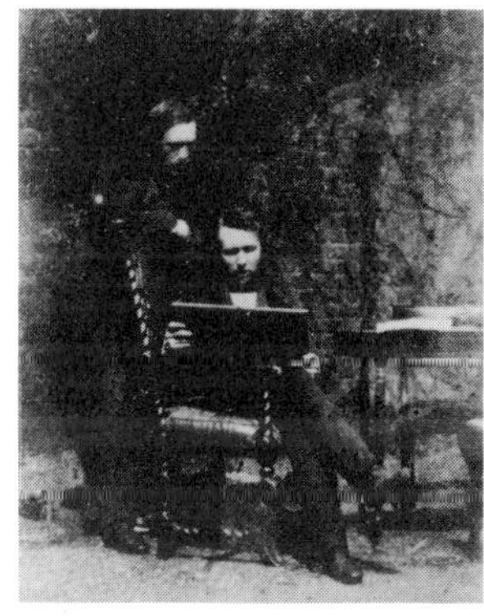

Fig 5 John Muir Wood
Charles Cundell and James Eckford Lauder, about 1847
salt print from a calotype negative
Scottish National Portrait Gallery

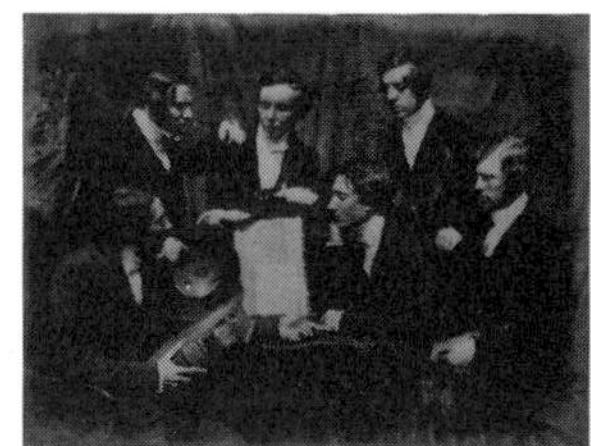

Fig 6 D O Hill and Robert Adamson
Professor Alexander Campbell Fraser and class, 1846
salt print from a calotype negative
Scottish National Portrait Gallery

Wood explored photographic lighting and printing using sculpture as his model. James Eckford Lauder's album of Wood's photographs includes the bust of Bacchus which Wood used for a series of studies (plates 5 to 8). He may have been acting on advice from Lauder or following WHF Talbot's example in *The Pencil of Nature*, which was published in 1844. In this, Talbot used a sculpted head of Patroclus (fig 9) in a similar experimental way:

> These delineations are susceptible of an almost unlimited variety: since in the first place, a statue may be placed in any position with regard to the sun, either directly opposite to it or at any angle: the directness or obliquity of the illumination causing of course an immense difference in the effect. And when a choice has been made of the direction in which the sun's rays shall fall, the statue may then be turned round on its pedestal, which produces a second set of variations no less considerable than the first.[21]

The same interest in experimental lighting is found also in Wood's portraits. For example in plate 40, he was concerned with creating the illusion that the candle was the light source in the picture. In fact, the photograph was taken out of doors in bright daylight and the candle flame, which would not have been visible, must have been drawn in on the negative. An artificial light source, perhaps a mirror, was set up to light the figure from the left, to achieve the effect of candlelight. A more exaggerated version of this idea is the portrait of a man (plate 39), posed indoors beside a window. Again the desired effect is a 'Caravaggist' one in which forms emerge dramatically, partially lit by the strong sunlight, part obscured in shadow.

A Photographic Tour

Most of the portraits and groups probably date from the 1840s when Wood was living in Edinburgh, and could well be his earliest work. There was only one occasion on which Wood recorded taking photographs, on his trip to the Continent in the summer of 1847. In July of that year, Wood left Edinburgh and headed for York. His diary for 19 July reads, 'Took views in York' (plates 48 and 49). His photographs emphasised the gothic character of the medieval city with dark, narrow streets and only the towers of the Minster visible in the unfocussed distance. After a few nights in London, one of which was spent at the opera, *The Marriage of Figaro*, with 'Mr Lauder', he left for Ostend on 28 July. There he lunched at the 'inconscionable' (dreadful) Hotel de Suede, where he 'paid for Camera — an imposition', and arrived at Bruges that evening.

His photographs of Bruges were taken on 29 July, or very early on the following morning, as he was in Ghent by 12.30. The stillness of the water and the clear reflections in his view of the Groene Rei (plate 11) would suggest that the photograph was taken at a time when nobody else was about. The photograph is a good demonstration of Wood's ability to think in monochrome, or, more specifically, in terms of light and dark. The composition is based on a balance of opposites: solid shapes on the left and broken shapes on the right; light and empty above and dark and crowded below. Wood strengthened, or possibly even added, the tree just to the left of the bridge to echo the spires and chimneys and their exaggerated reflections on the other side of the water.

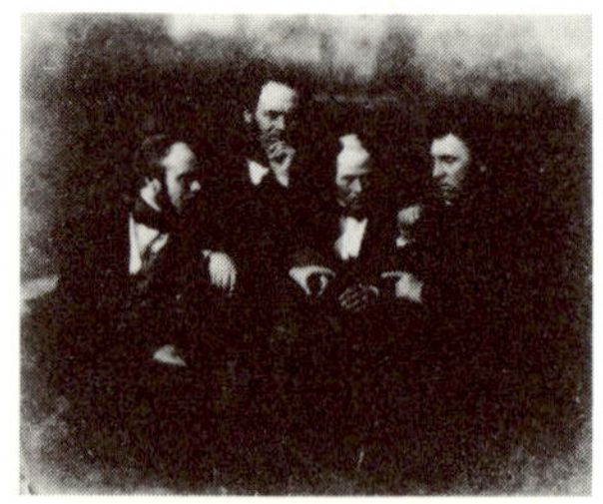

Fig 7 John Muir Wood
Group with Rev Robert Inglis (left) and George Wood (right), about 1847
salt print from a calotype negative
Scottish National Portrait Gallery

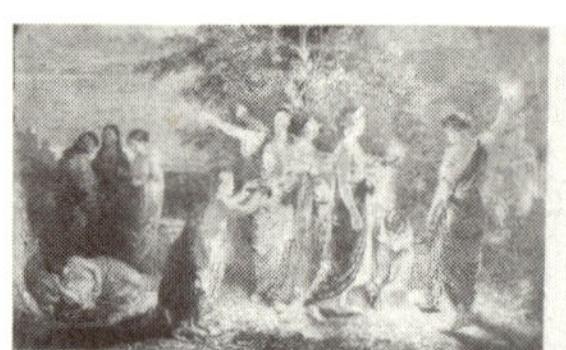

Fig 8 James Eckford Lauder
The Parable of the Ten Virgins
Engraving calotyped by J M Wood
Scottish National Portrait Gallery

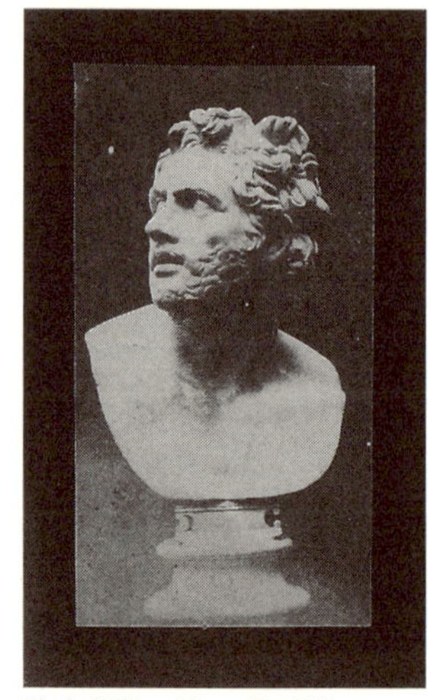

Fig 9 William Henry Fox Talbot
Bust of Patroclus LA 838
salt print from a calotype negative
Lacock Abbey Collection

21 H Fox Talbot, *The Pencil of Nature*, London, 1844, notes to plate v.

In Ghent, he 'Took views of La Maison des Bateliers — the Count of Flandres' Castle partly a manufactory [and the] Church of S. Jacques' (fig 10). This is one of Wood's most adventurous photographs. He deliberately stood back to include the striped awnings which break arbitrarily through the picture frame and, in doing so, took the risk of a gust of wind agitating them and ruining the photograph. Wood was not the only photographer abroad in Ghent that day. He commented, 'Met with 3 *agreeable* Englishmen, Snell, Charles and Wm H Barry, all architects apparently: the first sketching, the 2nd Calotyping; got detail of his process & showed mine; his w[or]k: sharp but bad in colour & would not print out well.' Wood probably spent the following day, 31 July, calotyping with the architects. His diary entry reads: 'Took the old Hotel de Ville — a fine Gothic building, the north facade in the Spanish gothic; the eastern one in three tiers of three different orders, Roman Doric, Ionic, & Corinthian — bad — the churches very uninteresting on the outsides'. On 2 August, Wood was calotyping in Mechelen: 'took views — prepared paper in a room slightly obscured by a green curtain — Tried Barry's process.' It is interesting that Wood was prepared to try a process he was sceptical about. One negative (plate 12) taken in Mechelen has the reddish colour which would not print well and Wood may not have even tried to print from it. Another photograph taken in Mechelen (plate 13) was, however, successful. Wood then moved on to Brussels where he visited the 'exposition de l'industrie' with Robert Frain and Alexander Christie, two Scottish painters.[22]

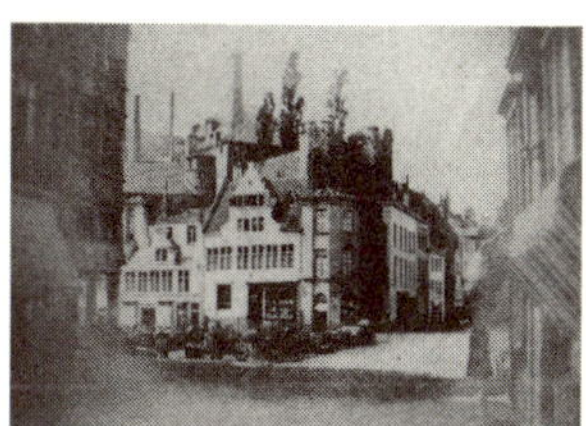

Fig 10 John Muir Wood
Ghent, 1847
salt print from a calotype negative
Scottish National Portrait Gallery

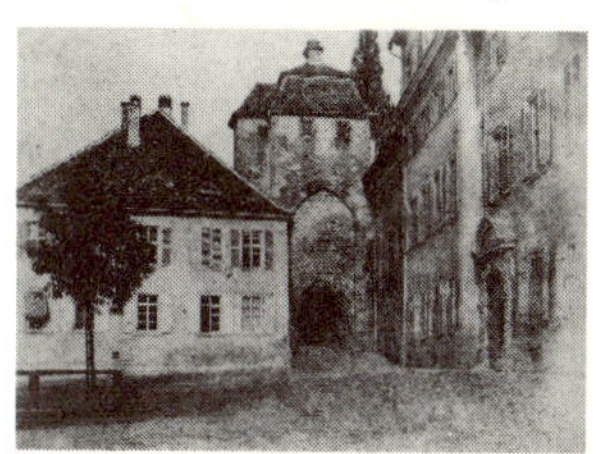

Fig 11 John Muir Wood
German town, perhaps 1847
salt print from a calotype negative
Scottish National Portrait Gallery

After visiting the field of Waterloo, he left for Namur which he declared to be 'not interesting'. This dismissive remark is more important than it sounds. Wood took a photograph in Namur which is, both in the negative and in the positive, one of his most beautiful images (cover plates). He thought of the town as unattractive, and the ordinary tourist, who expects to be provided with the picturesque view rather than to make his own picture, would at this point have put his camera away. Wood, however, brought to the town his own understanding of what makes a successful photograph. By including the incidental features like the passing barges on the river and the poles jutting out over the water in a strong architectural composition, he created a highly atmospheric picture. On Sunday 8 August, he 'descended the Meuse by steam to Liege', where he attended church and photographed the Palais de Justice.

The diary ends here, so we cannot be certain whether or not he returned to Britain at this point. It seems likely that he continued into Germany, where he took photographs in Cologne, Heidelberg, Nuremberg and Munich (plates 51 to 54). Some of these photographs are similar in character to his townscapes in York and Belgium — a response to the picturesque disorder of medieval towns. He carried through the idea of giving a glimpse of a gothic cathedral just appearing at the end of a dark street in York, and seen like a distant mountain over rooftops or across the river in Cologne (plates 51 and 52). But some of his German photographs, such as fig 11, have a quality of direct simplicity, and the quietude and geometric precision associated with classical art. He was not unmoved by neo-classical elegance, which appears in his photograph of Alexander Nasmyth's little classical temple, St Bernard's Well (plate 47), set beside the Water of Leith in Edinburgh. The differences between subjects, marked by a difference in approach, reflect the sophistication and catholicity of taste of a man who appreciated Bach and Beethoven, Mozart and Chopin.

22 Robert Frain (fl. 1840s-1870), portrait painter; Alexander Christie (1807-1860), Director of the Trustees' Academy in Edinburgh.

Melrose Abbey

Wood's approach to architecture can be seen particularly well in the series of forty-eight photographs he took of Melrose Abbey. The Wood family had friends living at Marlefield House, close to Melrose, which would have enabled him to spend time considering and photographing the Abbey. This group of photographs is the clearest evidence of Wood educating himself in the understanding of his subject. In later years, he visited several of the English cathedrals and there is an echo of his intention at Melrose in a letter he wrote to his wife: 'Really to do these Cathedrals justice, one should stay two or three days in each place, and become familiar with the style of each: as it is, I am jumbling them up in my head, without being quite sure where I saw a particular feature.' The photographs he took at Melrose include straightforward pictures of the whole building (fig 12) and the more personal photographs (plates 19 to 21) where he was making his own adventurous compositions. Wood made a number of direct photographs of architecture to prompt his memory or to help him learn more about buildings, in a way characteristic of the respectful approach of the photographers of architecture in the 1840s and 1850s. But he continued to take a different photographic interest in architecture. He visited Stonehenge in 1871 and was prompted to say, 'rather disappointing at first, till you examine the proportions — I wished very much for my camera, for I could have got some fine subjects.' This remark, which is similar to his reaction to Namur, supports the idea that in the Melrose photographs and, (as will be seen later), in his landscape photographs, we can see a man who is first reacting to a building or a view in a simple way — disliking or being impressed by it as it is — and *then* taking the time to allow his intelligence and feelings for a place to make a new and expressive idea from it.

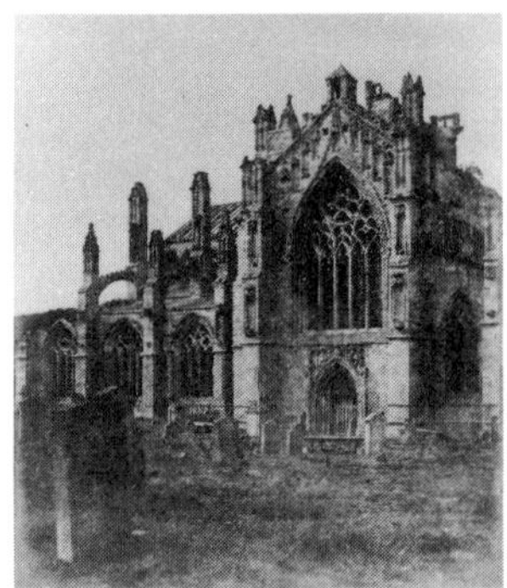

Fig 12 John Muir Wood
Melrose Abbey
salt print from a calotype negative
Scottish National Portrait Gallery

Romanticism and Nationalism

Wood's education in Germany, reinforced by his visits to catch up with contemporary music in 1835 and 1836, enabled him to see Scotland in a manner close to John Stuart Blackie who was the Edinburgh Professor of Classics in the 1840s. Blackie, like Wood, received his academic education in Germany. His biography referred to a walking tour he took in Scotland in 1836 as having 'roused to a very marked degree the stirrings of his nature, which were sacred to Scottish influences and to Scottish associations. If Germany made a conquest of his mind, his heart belonged then and always to Scotland.'[23]

The two men had in common an interest in Scottish music. Blackie wrote a book on Scottish songs, which referred to Wood in the preface as one of his musical mentors. He saw the popular songs of Scotland as an expression of the spirit of the people, believing that the heart of a national culture and a national identity are to be located in the folk music of a people. He said that, 'The songs that please the great mass of the people are the songs that flowed most directly and most potently from the people: and whosoever wishes to know the people, must know to love their songs.' He believed that, 'The purely native, patriotic and natural element' is found uniquely, 'in the sphere of the popular song or "Volkslied", a domain of musical expression which has peculiar claims on our attention, as retaining those charms of native growth, native atmosphere, native incident and native heroism, from which the higher branches of the art have so unfortunately been divorced.'[24] The impulse that underlies the collecting and collating of Wood's *Songs of Scotland* was, in Blackie's terms, nationalistic or patriotic.

23 Anna M Stoddart, *John Stuart Blackie. A biography*, Edinburgh and London, (no date), p 114.

24 John Stuart Blackie, *Scottish Songs*, Edinburgh, 1889, preface.

There is no doubt that Wood was a patriot and that his photographs of the Scottish landscape are those of, 'an enthusiast in taking views of the scenery of his beloved native land.'[25] Wood, like Blackie, responded to the Scottish landscape as a direct physical source of inspiration. Blackie's biography recounts, 'Marching alone down the glens and up the mountains, his faculties quickened by movement in the fresh and heather-sweetened air, he covered much ground in his wanderings. As he walked he sang and shouted his lays into shape, aided rather than diverted by the shifting scenes of nature in her solitudes, or of peasant life and industry ...'[26] Blackie was an extrovert who talked about these experiences, unlike the more reticent Wood, whose diary recorded walking tours of Scotland nearly in shorthand: 'Wed. 16: To Kingshouse — through a very [word missing] country — not a sheep or a house — Lochs Lyndoch — Eroch — Rannoch — Devils Staircase leads to Fort Augustus — through Glencoe — awfully grand — seems volcanic — The Cona[?] — Loch Leven — Ballachulish — Portnacroish — Appin — Skian ferry — Beregonium — Conell ferry — Oban — no bed ½ past one am. Walked 38m: Drove 16 — Ferry 3'. The following day, he and his friends covered a distance of 120 miles by sea. This was not ordinary tourist behaviour. That Wood's emotions were strongly involved in the country he explored comes to us at second hand from a letter to him by his friend Robert Inglis (plate 10), responding cynically to an account of a similar tour in 1831: 'Britha Jock in his last letter gives me a pompous and Jack-the-Giant-Killer like account of an expedition which you and he have had ... of seeing as much from some outlandish place, which he calls the Ochills, as the Yorkshire man saw at the Shows in Piccadilly ... you who it seems can travel 30 miles per diem.'

Although Wood's strength of feeling for his country clearly came from direct experience, his response was also conditioned by his education in Europe. When talking about poetry, emotion and the Romantic landscape, the European countries, especially Germany and France, thought of Scotland. Wood's experience in France in the 1820s led him to appreciate the Romantic advantage of being Scots: 'I am convinced more and more each day that the French hate the English mortally ... In going into company I contrive to let them know I am a Scotchman, for Mary Stuart [Mary, Queen of Scots] seems to be a saving clause, a kind of link between the two nations, which places us more on a footing, and at the same time by recalling the cruelty of Elizabeth, gratifies the French who have an opportunity of launching out in a philippic against the English.'

Thirty years later, the Romantic view of Scotland was still strong in France. The critic, Ernest Lacan, published in 1856 a series of 'Photographic Sketches' (*Esquisses Photographiques*), describing and categorising the different photographers. He chose Edouard-Denis Baldus as representative of the poetic photographers: 'If you are a poet, if you like the grand aspects of Nature ... follow Monsieur Baldus to the sublime country of the Auvergne ... each of his prints is a poem, sometimes wild, imposing, fantastic, like a page of Ossian; sometimes calm, melancholy, harmonious, like a meditation by Lamartine ... This sinister place is inhabited, in popular superstition, by dark and dismal figures. You almost see the ghost of King Lear or the skeletal shape of the witch from Macbeth.'[27]

In describing the work of a French photographer photographing the

25 Obituary of John Muir Wood, *The Musical Herald*, 1 August 1892.

26 Anna M Stoddart, op.cit., p 207, referring to Blackie's *Braemar Ballads*, published in 1857.

27 Ernest Lacan, *Esquisses Photographiques*, Paris, 1856 (reprinted 1986), p 27.

French landscape, two of the poetic references that came to Lacan's mind were Scottish. Elsewhere he refers to James Thomson's *The Seasons*. The European habit of referring to Scotland came from four major sources: James Macpherson's poems of Ossian, James Thomson, Robert Burns, and Sir Walter Scott.

All four poets have in common a habit of associating the Scottish landscape with human history. Burns and Scott were most specific in locating historic (whether fictional or real) events in particular places, so clearly identified that their readers could visit the sites of *The Lady of the Lake*, or the very place where Burns met Highland Mary, and relive the stories in their own minds. Chauncy Hare Townshend, who was one of the tourists in Scotland in the 1840s, was typical of many. Passing through the scenery of Scott's novels, he was continually reminded of whole dramatic passages. On seeing the rock from which Morris was thrown to his death at the command of Helen MacGregor in the novel, *Rob Roy*, he said, 'We could not but vividly recall that magnificent description of the coward's death agony — the unavailing struggle — the sudden plunge...'[28]

It was not simply the tourists but also the painters who haunted the literary landscape. David Octavius Hill painted a series of pictures, engraved and published in 1840 as *The Land of Burns* (fig 13).[29] It is no coincidence that the first book of photographs to be published on one subject, in 1845, was WHF Talbot's *Sun Pictures in Scotland*, which was devoted to scenes associated with Walter Scott. John Muir Wood explored the south-west of Scotland, where Burns lived and was inspired to write many of his greatest poems, and the Borders which Scott made his home.

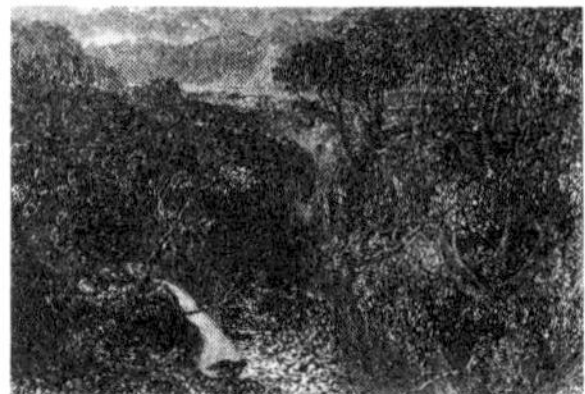
Fig 13 David Octavius Hill
The Fall of Foyers
engraving after oil painting, published 1840
Private collection

Wood's photographs of Melrose Abbey (plates 19 to 21) undoubtedly reflect Scott's enthusiasm for the place, expressed in his poem, *The Lay of the Last Minstrel*:

The moon on the east oriel shone,
Through slender shafts of shapely stone,
By foliaged tracery combined:
Then wouldst thou have thought some fairy's hand
Twixt poplars straight the osier wand
In many a freakish knot had twined;
Then framed a spell, when the work was done,
And changed the willow wreaths to stone.

Scott's verse treated the ruins of Melrose as part of nature and Wood's approach to the building echoes this feeling. Plates 19 and 20 are similar in composition to his views of woodland, with stone columns replacing the trees. The analogy between Melrose and the geology of Staffa is irresistible (plate 66): the natural basalt columns bearing up the rough, crushed rocks above — the building of the Ossianic giants; the carved gothic columns supporting the equally rough ruined masonry in Melrose — both the natural and the man-made becoming objects of religious awe. Plate 19 is one of several cases where Wood's negatives have an individual and beautiful life of their own. The swirling mist apparently drifting through was an effect of nature that photography was not yet capable of capturing. In the photograph it is an accident caused in floating the paper onto imperfectly-mixed chemicals: the result is nonetheless strangely attractive and suggestive of Scott's fantasy.

28 Chauncy Hare Townshend, *A Descriptive Tour in Scotland*, London, 1846, p 27.

29 'At a comparatively early stage of his career he suggested to Messrs Blackie, publishers, Glasgow, a publication under the title of "The Land of Burns", for which he subsequently executed a series of 60 landscapes, illustrative of the scenes which the bard had immortalised. It was suggested that these pictures should be preserved as a public collection somewhere on the banks of Doon, but for want of funds the proposal fell through, and one half of the series has since been destroyed by fire.' Obituary of D O Hill, *Scotsman*, 17 May 1870.

The eighteenth-century poems of Ossian were supposed to be ancient Celtic legends of heroism, love and death, and described a Scottish landscape redolent of heroic emotion, but generalised in character. Amongst Wood's contemporaries, the judge, Lord Jeffrey, was one who thought of the real landscape in these imaginative terms. He described the Highlands of Scotland as, 'ample solitudes of unploughed and untrodden valleys, — nameless and gigantic ruins, — and mountain echoes repeating the scream of the eagle and the roar of the cataract. It is sympathy with the present or the past, or the imaginary inhabitants of such a region, that alone gives it either interest or beauty; and the delight of those who behold it, will always be found to be in exact proportion to the force of their imaginations, and the warmth of their social affections.'[30] Wood himself referred to Ossian in his discussions of ancient Gaelic music in the following terms: 'The Ossianic chants are short and wild ... formless and uninteresting as mere music. From these emerge airs still wild and irregular, but with a certain sublimity arising from their very vagueness.'[31] This description seems to fit some of Wood's most interesting, and arguably his most difficult, photographs (for example, plates 23 and 24).

Landscape and the Calotype Process

Most of John Muir Wood's landscapes may be seen in terms of the established conventions of landscape painting, of which he evidently had a sophisticated understanding. The scene is presented to the viewer in a way that invites him to enter and pass through it as an imaginative journey. The formal method of achieving this effect was to include a path or stream that leads the eye into the picture. There is generally a particular area of focus, as in plate 36, in which the ruined building on the brow of the hill, with its suggestion of a once-inhabited place, adds poignancy. The concept of the picturesque, expressed by Uvedale Price as 'the disposition of objects which by a partial and uncertain concealment excites and nourishes the curiosity',[32] is applicable to many of Wood's landscapes and to his medieval townscapes. The figures illustrating the 1842 edition of Price's book on picturesque landscape gardening (fig 14) are similar to many of the photographs. It is, therefore, all the more interesting that in several of his landscape photographs Wood departed from the familiar conventions and made pictures of surprising originality and intensity. These photographs are his personal response to the place. They are unconventional in their composition: the eye is not led easily through the picture and the viewer is not invited to follow a path or a stream. We glimpse a dark and mysterious place, which we can look at but not enter (plates 23, 24, 29 and 31).

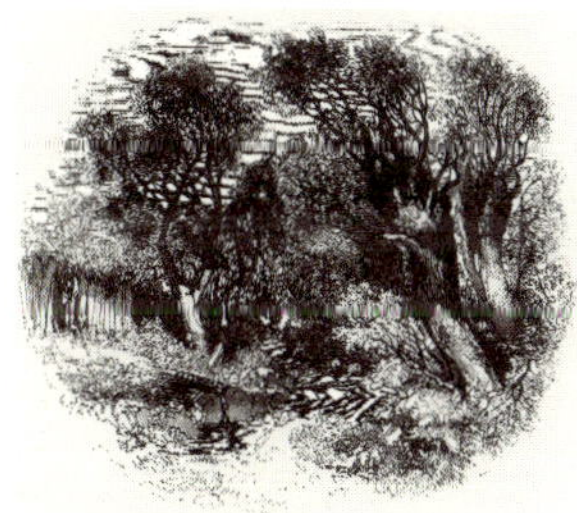

Fig 14 Montagu Stanley
Illustration to Uvedale Price, *On the Picturesque*, 1842 edition

This combination of the private and the mysterious has an interesting parallel with Wood's musical experience. One member of the audience at the concert organised by Wood for Chopin in 1848 described Chopin's music as 'strange, fantastic, wandering, incomprehensible, but less fitted, on the whole, for the popular concert hall than for the salon of a private mansion.'[33] Wood's photographs embody one of the vital insights of the Romantic sensibility — the connection between music and landscape.

There is a sense in which these woodland photographs are peculiarly without subject matter. That is, there is no desire on the part of the photographer to

30 Francis Jeffrey, quoted in Sir Thomas Dick Lauder's introductory essay, 'On the origin of taste', to Sir Uvedale Price, *On the Picturesque*, Edinburgh and London, 1842, p 10.

31 J M Wood, 'Scotish [*sic*] Music', in George Grove, *Dictionary of Music and Musicians*, vol 3, p 448.

32 Uvedale Price, op.cit., p69.

33 Sir James Hedderwick quoted in A E Bone, *Jane Wilhelmina Stirling 1804-1859*, 1960, p 74.

name the place or specify the scene. The subject becomes the occasion for sensation, and the result is a single, poetic idea. An imprecise and generalising process, the calotype lent itself particularly well to this way of seeing. As in the paintings of J M W Turner, where structure and detail were sacrificed, lost in his 'amber-coloured ether' for the sake of conveying atmosphere and mood in a single, unified vision, so the calotype conveyed total effects rather than discrete elements.

There is a sensuous, lively pleasure to be had from the calotype process which is distinct from the precise miniature charm of the daguerreotype. The slightly coarse effect of the image, filtered through a paper negative and carried by the chemicals into the fibre of the paper print, gave the calotype a quality of movement and of life. D O Hill was especially attracted by this character: 'The rough surface & unequal texture throughout the paper is the main cause of the calotype failing in details before the process of Dageurrotypes — & this is the very life of it. They look like the imperfect work of a man and not the much diminished perfect work of God.'[34] The calotype photographers were using the same kind of paper (most importantly, Whatman's Turkey Mill) which the watercolour painters had discovered about twenty years earlier. The blurring of the colour into the paper and the white of the paper itself gave an effect of the paper containing and giving out its own light rather than merely reflecting light. This was the effect which Turner exploited with such skill. The 'richness of surface' admired by the painters was combined in the calotype process with a subtlety of chemical reaction. The calotype was one of the 'printing-out' processes, that is to say the print remained in contact with the negative whilst it developed in the sunshine rather than being chemically developed out after a short exposure. The dark areas of the negative helped to mask the light areas of the print while the picture developed, registering a wide range of detail in all areas of the print. This made it possible for John Muir Wood to take successful photographs in such technically challenging conditions as sun-streaked woodland.

Wood's calotypes are particularly remarkable for their colour. Robert Adamson was capable of keeping the process to a fairly close range of a dense, reddish or purple brown but his control was unusual. G S Cundell's description of the calotype said: 'In these pictures there is a curious and beautiful variety in the tints of colour they will occasionally assume, varying from a rich golden orange to purple and black.'[35] Wood's colours have an element of accident about them — during experiments he found particular colours, and his rich purple print of tangled undergrowth is conceivably one of these happy discoveries — but it is also clear that he found this extraordinary variety of colour because he enjoyed it and because he was looking for it. His chemical experimentation and his use of different papers had this end in sight. His discovery of colour and the subtle reaction of the calotype process gave his work its essentially lyrical character. His few attempts to work in the later carbon process (plate 34), which was coloured by a dye rather than by a chemical reaction, are much flatter and less attractive than his earlier work.

Wood's approach to the calotype process may reasonably be related to his knowledge of music. A parallel can be drawn between the ideas of theme and variation, or the concept that music is different at each performance, and his readiness to experiment with varieties of different printing. The parallel can be taken further. Wood's

34 Letter from D O Hill to Elhanan Bicknell, 17 January 1848, ms in the collection of George Eastman House.

35 George Smith Cundell, 'On the practice of the Calotype Process of Photography', *The London, Edinburgh and Dublin Philosophical Magazine and Journal of Science*, May 1844, p 331.

approach to the 'truth' of photography was not scientific, but closer to the poetic idea of truth; that it can be worked on, raised and idealised. Just as there may be no perfect response to a musical score, there need be no single interpretation of a photographic negative. Wood on occasion made as many as six different kinds of print from one negative, altering the character of the image with each one. In this he differed again from D O Hill and Robert Adamson. Hill who was a painter of poetic landscape had a respect for the truth of the calotype which stopped him from interfering unnecessarily with the negative or the print. Hill and Adamson composed their calotypes through the camera, did not cut or extend the photographs during printing and confined their touching up of the negative to reinforcing lines or removing chemical spots. Their manipulation took place in front of the camera, so that any untruth they persuaded it to tell by, for example, altering the lighting or devising a more dignified pose, was still a photographic truth. This is all the more remarkable because the calotype, whose negative and positive were both on drawing paper, was an open temptation to retouching and improvement. Wood composed and constructed his calotypes almost as much out of the camera as in it. He cut his photographs to different shapes, he added extra paper to the negative to make more sky, he painted in leaves and plants, he painted out obtrusive trees or branches (in plate 65), he changed the lines of hills (in plate 33), and even added a small mountain range to the view from his Edinburgh windows.

Composition

One of the serious problems of early photography was that it flattened distance and could not register the bright sky at the same time as the dark land. This explains why D O Hill whose landscape painting was dependent on an affection for 'aerial perspective', which is distance seen through atmospheric light, was not notably interested in landscape photography. His most successful landscape photographs were close-ups (fig 15), using an exaggerated bounced light and a short focal range.

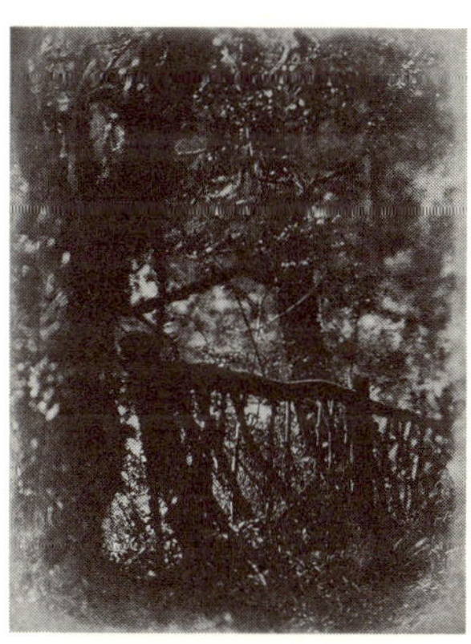

Fig 15 D O Hill and Robert Adamson
Tree and fence, 1846
salt print from a calotype negative
Scottish National Portrait Gallery

Wood approached this problem in several ways. He tried decorating the blank white skies by drawing in clouds. In photographs like plate 59, he used the curious cut-out effect deliberately by composing his picture in abrupt transitions from dark into light and from near into distance — with a result not unlike a peep-show. He also achieved a greater sense of perspective and depth by marking the space out physically with tree trunks, paths or the flow of water (plates 63 and 64), or he deliberately closed in the photograph and reversed the idea of aerial perspective by making the dark spaces create the depth in the picture (plates 29 and 31). In even simpler photographs he reduced his view to a silhouetted pattern of trees in a single plane (plates 35 and 62). His landscape photographs were by turns theatrical, mysterious or simply decorative rather than truthful. It may be that as a student of music, an abstract art form, he liked effects that his contemporaries might well have found reductive and false.

Occasionally, Wood's photographs are eccentric in their composition. A principle of variety, asymmetry, even dissonance underlies pictures like 'Canterbury' (plate 50) and 'Tighnabruich' (plate 25). Each has the appearance of two separate photographs combined, with the right and left sides different in character. In 'Tighnabruich' the effect is created because on the left a tree is silhouetted against the light, a strong flat shape that dominates the photograph. On the right- hand side a road leads away into a deep perspective, creating a sense of distance and space; the two halves of the composition are contradictory.

'Canterbury' is also made up of oppositions: of light and dark, open and closed forms, solid and void. There is a multiplicity of elements: textural, anecdotal, architectural. The solid brick wall in the foreground finds its visual antithesis in the pierced Norman windows and archway. Although figures are introduced, they do not relate to each other in any clear way. The cumulative effect of so many disparate elements is one of dislocation. The same sense of dislocation can be found in the groups like 'A game of bowls' (plate 37) where the figures are divided between the two sides of the picture. This sense is even greater in other groups where there is no focus of interest and the figures are strung out across the composition. This, of course, reflects the difficulty of making groups appear natural, which was a perennial problem for photographers as with would-be 'naturalist' painters.

The question prompted by such photographs is, to what extent are these effects calculated and to what extent are they accidental. If accidental, they are happy accidents, for these photographs are successful despite their unorthodoxy. The work of an amateur, using the unpredictable new medium of photography, must carry a doubt about the photographer's intention. But to be an amateur is not necessarily to be less of an artist. Wood's photography certainly involves accident, but his reaction to these accidents was receptive and creative.

Science, Art and Photography

From the perspective of the twentieth century, the invention of photography was one of the classic watersheds of history — one of those discoveries that altered habits of thought and affected intellectual progress. Before the camera could capture its own images on chemically-impregnated paper or sensitised metal, science and art were interlocked, the subjects of a forced marriage. This idea can be seen in the dependence of the scientists on the manipulative skill of the artists to convey their meaning to the world. Particularly in publications, the scientist required draughtsmen of sufficient ability to produce acceptable illustrations of nature, machinery, landscape and so forth. Certain complex ideas, like the classification of plants, could only be communicated by eye; a buttercup or an elm tree may be described in detail but a clear mental image can only be transmitted through a picture.

Analytical, scientific or historic works were therefore dependent not just on the skill of the artist but also on his own individual approach to the author's subject — in the painter's or engraver's hands, a book might subtly change subject. As an example, one book whose illustrations bear a strong resemblance to certain of John Muir Wood's landscape photographs (plate 36), was *The Provincial Antiquities of Scotland*, written by Sir Walter Scott and illustrated by Rev John Thomson and J M W Turner.[36] The title is clear enough; this was to be a book about historical monuments. But Thomson and Turner were both painters who had adopted the associative idea of landscape — the idea that the landscape itself was as redolent of the history of man as the visible ruins left by his passing. In *The Provincial Antiquities*, this resulted in a series of illustrations of landscape which included, as subordinate (and in two cases, nearly invisible)

36 Sir Walter Scott, *The Provincial Antiquities of Scotland*, London, 1819-1826.

features, the antiquities of the title. This situation becomes even stranger, when we take into account a remark made by Scott, who greatly admired John Thomson's painting, that the landscape in his painting of Crichton Castle (fig 16) was more imaginative than real.[37]

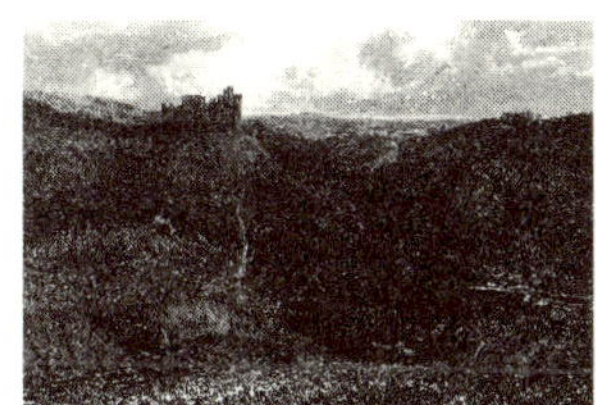

Fig 16 Rev John Thomson
Crichton Castle
engraving for Sir Walter Scott's *The Provincial Antiquities of Scotland*, 1819-1826
National Gallery of Scotland

It would, however, be a mistake to see the association of science and art in the early nineteenth century as a hostile or unhappy one. They were linked together in theory as well as practice and shared the same concept of Romanticism that the truth lay in a close study of nature and of detail. The physicist Sir David Brewster, who was irritated by much in the artists' way of thinking, pursued his own researches in a loving, enthusiastic manner: 'a constant observing and experimenting upon some common daily occurence — the colours and forms of plants, the eye balls of fish and other creatures, the habits of gold-fish, the gambols of mice ... the scratching of snail shells on the window, the jewels and tinted ribbons of his lady visitors ...'[38] Brewster's manner of observation was no different from that of Sir Walter Scott, examining a location for his novel, *Rokeby.* J B S Morritt witnessed Scott at work, 'noting down even the peculiar little wild flowers and herbs that accidentally grew round and on the side of a bold crag near his intended cave of Guy Denzil; and could not help saying, that as he was not to be upon oath in his work, daisies, violets, and primroses would be as poetical as any of the humble plants he was examining... but I understood him when he replied, that in nature herself no two scenes were exactly alike, and that whoever copied truly what was before his eyes, would possess the same variety in his descriptions, and exhibit apparently an imagination as boundless as the range of nature in the scenes he recorded; whereas whoever trusted to imagination, would soon find his own mind circumscribed, and contracted to a few favourite images, and the repetition of these would sooner or later produce that very monotony and barrenness which had always haunted descriptive poetry in the hands of any but the patient worshippers of truth.'[39]

This same scrupulous attitude to truth can be found in such publications as Wood's own work, *The Songs of Scotland*, a scholarly edition concerned to find the scientific, historical truth behind the most Romantic poetry.

The invention of photography was not, therefore, the discovery of a scientific tool to liberate the scientist from the damp clasp of the artist but the discovery of a new method of examining the world of driving interest to both. Talbot thought that photography would extend rather than limit the role of the artist, making him more dependent on a knowledge of chemistry and physics: 'I remember it was said by many persons, at the time when photogenic drawing was first spoken of, that it was likely to prove injurious to art, as substituting mere mechanical labour in lieu of talent and experience. Now, so far from this being the case, I find that in this, as in most other things, there is ample room for the exercise of skill and judgement. It would hardly be believed how different an effect is produced by a longer or shorter exposure to the light, and also, by mere variations in the fixing process, by means of which almost any tint, cold or warm, may be thrown over the picture ... All this falls within the artist's province to combine and to regulate; and if, in the course of these manipulations, he, *nolens volens*, becomes a chemist and an optician, I feel confident that such an alliance of science and art will prove conducive to the improvement both.'[40] Photography, in the event, did not limit or separate the roles of scientist and artist — it extended them. Men with

37 Letter from Walter Scott to Lady Abercorn, quoted in William Baird, *John Thomson of Duddingston*, Edinburgh, 1895, pp 88-89.

38 Mrs Gordon, *The Home Life of Sir David Brewster*, Edinburgh, 1869, p 302.

39 John Bacon Sawrey Morritt, quoted in J G Lockhart, *The Life of Sir Walter Scott, Bart,* London, 1893, p226.

40 W H F Talbot, letter to the editor, *The London, Edinburgh and Dublin Philosophical Magazine and Journal of Science,* July 1841, pp 89-90.

no skill to draw, like Talbot, could at last develop their aesthetic ability; men with no professional concern with chemistry, like John Muir Wood, could learn through photography to exploit its natural beauty. Talbot's remarks, quoted above, expressed in casual terms one of the most astonishing facts about photography: the 'independent', the 'objective' eye of the camera was no such thing. The idea that printing little pictures of reality was alchemy or magic rather than cold science was not just a poetic fancy. The camera proved to be a distorting mirror, with its own strange rules and unexpected accidents.

Ernest Lacan expressed this in musical terms which would have made sense to Wood, when answering the thoughtless critics of photography who still believed that making a photograph was a simple matter of standing the camera in front of a fine view: 'Anyone who puts this idea to the test will be swiftly disillusioned. The very best camera will not copy by itself a portrait, a view or a landscape, any more than the best Stradivarius or Érard [a piano] can play the slightest theme or the most simple motif by itself. The photographer, like the musician, like the painter, like the sculptor, needs two essential qualities: experience and feeling.'[41] By a curious inversion of likelihood, the newly-invented camera was an object that inspired its owners with poetic enthusiasm and the strongly personal, not objective, vision which is seen so effectively in the work of John Muir Wood.

Conclusion

John Muir Wood was an amateur. In the early years of photography this could be more an advantage than a disadvantage: the amateur was far freer than the professional, untrammelled by the need to make a living from a new and awkward art. The professional was obliged to concentrate on the simple practical problems of producing a consistent and reliable result, which could occupy most if not all of his time. His work would have been more tied to an idea of public demand — portraits or tourist views.

Wood was highly educated and sophisticated both in his knowledge of chemistry and in his experience and understanding of the visual arts. Much of his work can be linked to broad cultural movements in Scotland and in the rest of Europe.

He was not, however, merely repeating tried formulae. Art is a problem-solving activity, and the creative process involves continual decision-making. One of the unexpected virtues of photography, in view of its reputation as a mechanical art, is that critical choices can be made at any stage of the production of the final work. The element of accident is, however, of greater importance than in any other art form. The readiness to accept accidents and even to look for them, which is familiar in twentieth-century photography, was equally important to a few early photographers like John Muir Wood.

This was not the incompetence of amateurism, but its greatest asset. It can be seen in Wood's readiness to tackle difficulties rather than avoid them that he was laying himself open to the possibilities of accident. The early photographic processes were not capable of a direct reflection of the real world. The calotype was not an imitation but a translation of reality and photographers needed to master a visual language with an unexpected grammar.

41 Ernest Lacan, op.cit., p 77.

The key photograph amongst Wood's landscapes stands as a model of his originality (plate 23). Its colour is bizarre and its composition is eccentric, an unstructured tangle of undergrowth, which has exceeded the picturesque concept of natural landscape. Wood was an amateur, but a highly accomplished amateur; his was not an innocent eye but an open eye.

John Muir Wood and Photographic Chemistry
By Michael Gray

John Muir Wood's work presents a complex series of challenges that are difficult to define or analyse. In endeavouring to make comparisons or draw conclusions, an attempt must be made to relate his work to that of his contemporaries and to examine the technical and aesthetic context in which he practised the art of photography. In the first instance, John Muir Wood can clearly be regarded as one of the vanguard of the second wave of photographers, those who acquired practical knowledge of the calotype and salt printing processes without direct access to the inventor, William Henry Fox Talbot,[1] or his immediate associates.

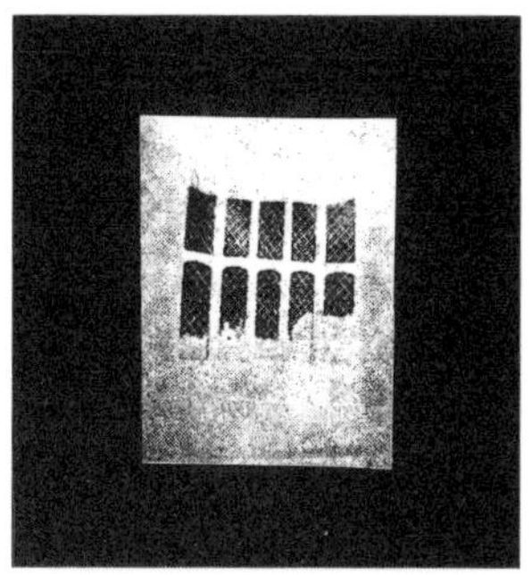

Fig 1 The Oriel Window, Lacock Abbey.

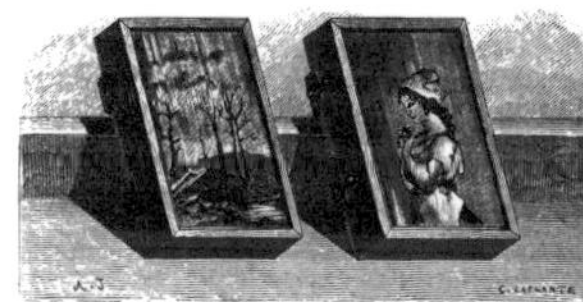

Fig 2 G Tissandier
A History of Photography

Photography on Paper 1834 to 1840

The photogenic drawing (or salt paper print) process: The first practical photographic process was known as photogenic drawing. In 1834, WHF Talbot of Lacock, Wiltshire, discovered that paper immersed in a weak solution of salt (sodium chloride) and then washed over with silver nitrate, formed silver chloride by double decomposition,[2] which was far more sensitive to light than silver nitrate. In 1835, using this basic method, he took the first known photographic negative of the oriel window in Lacock Abbey (fig 1). This was then stabilised with a strong solution of sodium chloride. He obtained a positive print by repeating this process in a printing frame (fig 2) with a further sheet of the same paper, and exposing it to the rays of the sun. This became the basic method of printing from negatives for the next sixty years until the introduction of chemical development.[3]

The photogenic drawing (or salt print) process was still relatively slow for negatives, the image being developed by the energy of sunlight alone. Talbot found a means of accelerating the process in September 1840.

The calotype: Talbot discovered that, if he used the same method of double decomposition to form a layer of silver iodide on his basic paper, a mixture of silver nitrate, acetic and gallic acid washed over the surface and exposed in the camera, whilst still wet, formed a highly sensitive surface. Exposures were then dramatically reduced, and although no image could be seen, a subsequent wash with the same sensitising solution developed the latent image.[4] This discovery established the structure of the modern photographic process in principle and practice.

Not until 1843, with the appearance of *Photographic Manipulation* published by Edward Palmer (fig 3), was a reliable description of the calotype process available to the public.[5] The unknown author gave clear workable instructions for the process with the first reference to the use of double iodide of silver, crediting a Mr Mitchell and Dr Ryan with its introduction. This soon became standard practice as

1 WHF Talbot (1800-1877) see HJP Arnold, *William Henry Fox Talbot Pioneer of photography and man of science*, London, 1977.

2 In this context silver nitrate ($AgNO_3$) in combination with sodium chloride (NaCl) gives, by exchange, silver chloride (AgCl) and sodium nitrate which takes no part in the reaction, thus the exchange or recombination, see Hardwich and Taylor, London, *Photographic Chemistry*, 1883, p 25.

3 In the printing out process the image is formed by the action of light on the silver halide, which converts or reduces the silver chloride to the metal and releases chlorine as a gas. This was a relatively slow method requiring strong sunlight and was superseded by the developing out process around the turn of the century.

it enabled a more even layer of the iodide of silver to be deposited on the paper. This article, in conjunction with George Smith Cundell's article in *The London, Edinburgh and Dublin Philosophical Journal*[6] published the following year, made the process available to amateurs. Given John Muir Wood's familiarity with the Cundell family it was probably the second source he would have drawn upon. It may reasonably be assumed that he took up calotype photography in 1844 or soon after.

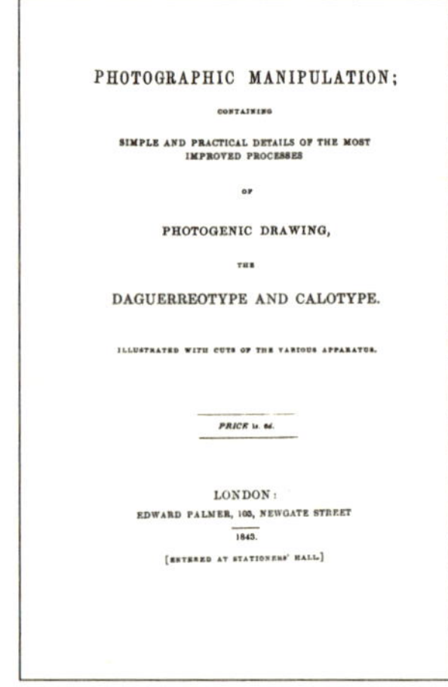
PHOTOGRAPHIC MANIPULATION;

CONTAINING

SIMPLE AND PRACTICAL DETAILS OF THE MOST IMPROVED PROCESSES

OF

PHOTOGENIC DRAWING,

THE

DAGUERREOTYPE AND CALOTYPE.

ILLUSTRATED WITH CUTS OF THE VARIOUS APPARATUS.

PRICE 1s. 6d.

LONDON:
EDWARD PALMER, 103, NEWGATE STREET
1843.
[ENTERED AT STATIONERS' HALL.]

Fig 3 E Palmer
Photographic Manipulation, 1843
Title page
Fox Talbot Museum

The Calotype Negatives of John Muir Wood

There is considerable variation in the quality and condition of John Muir Wood's surviving negatives. Their quality may be judged from the colour and contemporary observations relating to the coloration still hold true. Negatives that developed with fiery red characteristics such as plate 12, were judged to be technically inferior, whilst those that attained a deep rich black *ton noir gravure* were praised for their vigour and strength. Where Wood's negatives are blood-red in colour but not waxed to help stabilise them, they have faded, as can clearly be seen by the strength of the surviving retouching in plate 35. In some cases, Wood succeeded in taking an excellent print from a red negative (front cover) but the negative has since faded and is now deficient in detail and density (back cover). His best negatives were waxed and had deep, rich, black shadows. They remained stable and are still capable of producing fine prints, as is the case with the Melrose Abbey photographs (plates 19 and 20).

The tonal scale or density range of the calotype negative was much longer than its equivalent on film or glass. Salt paper had a much softer gradation of tones, but had limited potential for contrast control in the print. The onus was on the photographer to produce a perfect printing negative.

Wood's decision to wax a particular negative, was based on the overall technical quality of the image. A very good negative with a long tonal scale could safely be waxed to increase the transparency of the whites (the shadow areas of the print) whilst the strength of the blacks (or highlights) remained the same, or were marginally improved, by closing the paper fibres with the action of ironing with wax. Such a negative could stand printing in direct sunlight. However, a negative that was weak would, if waxed, gain nothing by becoming even more transparent.

Although Wood made prints from some of the unwaxed negatives other unwaxed negatives may not have been considered worth printing or capable of being printed. It must be remembered that there was virtually no flexibility in the printing-out process at this time and marginal changes to the tonal range were extremely difficult and rarely attempted. So these unwaxed, tonally deficient negatives may never have been put to the test. It was possible to achieve a level of technical excellence in the negative when all the circumstances were favourable, although skilled practitioners were, even in the late 1840s, subject to factors frequently beyond their control. All the classic technical faults found in modern photography can be seen in paper photography at this time: overexposure and underdevelopment; underexposure and overdevelopment. However, the problems faced by calotypists are difficult, today, to comprehend. The quality of the paper and chemicals were frequently suspect. The cost of experimenting was high. For example, hypo (sodium thiosulphate) for many years was 'six shillings a pound'[7], making it almost as expensive as the nitrate of silver.

4 See Beaumont Newhall, *The Latent Image*, Albuquerque, 1983, pp 112-138.

5 'WHT', *Photographic Manipulation*, London, 1843. The identity of the author of this pamphlet is unknown, although an obvious candidate would be Talbot himself, who sometimes signed himself WHT. Unfortunately, we must discount this possibility as the author refers to the work as 'a first literary attempt', and Talbot had already published many scientific articles.

6 George Smith Cundell, 'On the practice of the Calotype Process of Photography,' *The London, Edinburgh and Dublin Philosophical Magazine, and Journal of Science*, May 1844.

7 Thirty pence for 500 grams.

8 Thomas Augustus Malone was employed by WHF Talbot at the Reading Establishment in 1843. He later went into partnership with Nicolaas Henneman in London as 'Henneman and Malone'. For some years he kept in contact with Talbot and regularly corresponded with him on photographic matters. In the 1850s he was editor of *The British Journal of Photography*, and *The Liverpool and Manchester Photographic Journal*, and held posts at the Royal College of Chemistry and The Royal Polytechnic Institution.

Improvements in Paper

It became apparent towards the end of the 1840s that no further improvements could be achieved until a more suitable paper for making negatives was found. Like the other calotypists, John Muir Wood was at the mercy of the papermakers and his results varied considerably.

From the visible watermarks on his photographs, Wood tried at least ten different papers. Canson, Hollingworth, Turner, Whatman and other manufacturers made good papers, but still there were problems with uneven fibre distribution, grain, small particles of brass from buttons left in the cotton linters and minute pieces of iron from the beaters or calendering rollers. Even within the same make of paper, consistency could not be maintained without additional expense and the firm commitment of the mill owners. On the whole, papermakers regarded photographers until the early 1850s as somewhat of a nuisance. The potential market was small and the criteria for the elimination of contaminants were considered to be too stringent.

Thomas Augustus Malone[8] made numerous visits on behalf of WHF Talbot to Whatman's and R Turner's Mills at Maidstone to encourage improvements. His first recorded and apparently fruitless visit to a paper mill was noted in a letter to Talbot on 23 April 1848:

> I have seen the process for making paper at Whatmans and at Allnatts — both of Maidstone in Kent. Mr Hollingworth[9] the proprietor of Whatman's Mill advised me to go to see his friend Mr Allnatt[10] as he is fond of experimenting ... Mr Allnatt says a pure paper has not been made these 20 years — such as I described him.[11]

Two years later Malone and Nicolaas Henneman[12] made a contact which did produce concrete results. On 25 May 1850, a further communication to Talbot from Malone relates:

> It happens singularly that we have good news of the paper manufacturer Mr Turner and his brother of Chafford Mills (good makers) (fig 4) have been conversing with myself and Henneman and some Amateurs, his friends on the requisites for a good sheet of Photographic paper. They have already made improvements and promise they will not rest until much more has been accomplished.[13]

This initial contact led to the specification and production of a reliable base photographic paper which was to become available from 1852 onwards with the watermark 'R Turner Patent Talbotype'. This paper was of high quality and it was used by many photographers including Linnaeus Tripe, Benjamin Brecknell Turner, Rev T Melville Raven and Frederick Townshend.[14] John Muir Wood's negative of Dublin looking up the Liffey, was made on 'R Turner Patent Talbotype' (fig 5), and must, therefore, have been taken in 1852 or later.

John Muir Wood conducted extensive trials himself, on a wide range of papers. This can be verified by noting the variety of watermarks seen in both negative and positive images, (see cover photograph, plates 10, 15, 16, 17, 21, 29, 47, 53, 55, 56, 61, 65 and 66). By the mid 1850s he had achieved a high technical standard in the negative, enabling him to give more attention to printing and toning.

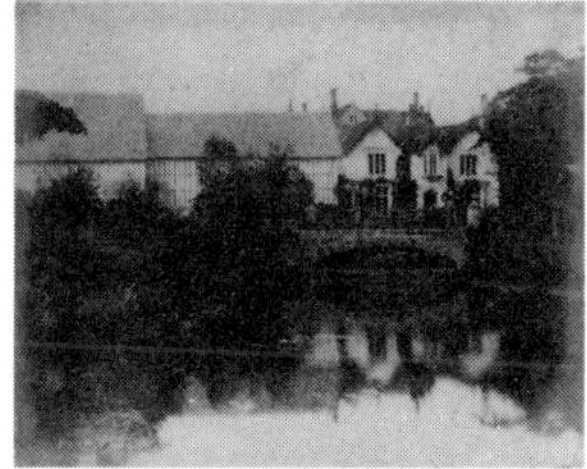

Fig 4 G Nicholson
Chafford Mills
salt print from a calotype negative
Scottish National Portrait Gallery

9 'Hollingsworth's Thin Photographic Paper' was so highly regarded that Thomas Sutton purchased a whole make of 40 reams, reported in *Photographic Notes, Journal of the Photographic Society of Scotland and of the Manchester Photographic Society*, 1856, pp 111 and 115.

10 Mr Allnatt, an associate of Mr Hollingsworth, could have met WHF Talbot as both were listed as being members of the Graphic Society in 1849. Lacock Abbey correspondence LA 48-49.

11 Lacock Abbey correspondence LA 48-25.

12 Nicolaas Henneman (1813-1898) was originally employed by Talbot as his valet, later assisting with early photographic experiments. In 1843 he was made responsible for setting up The Reading Establishment making prints for *The Pencil of Nature*. Henneman brought Thomas Malone to assist in the running of the works and, in 1848, they set up a portrait studio in Regent Street, London.

13 Lacock Abbey correspondence.

14 Townshend said that the Turner paper 'gives uniformly greater delicacy, sharpness and evenness than any of the foreign papers, and keeps perfectly in the gallic acid baths', 'On the Quality of Paper required for Photographic purposes, more particularly for the Waxed Paper Process', *Journal of the Photographic Society*, 1855, pp 166 and 167.

Printmaking and Reproduction: The circumstances influencing the contemporary perceptions of the photographic image at its introduction

Three printing processes, the mezzotint, aquatint and later the lithographic print, formed the language of vision which was to underpin and set the criteria by which photography was ultimately assessed. These established criteria were almost universally accepted by the critics and practitioners of the new medium of photography who had a knowledge of art. The ink-based printing processes were characterised by depth (the ink sank into the paper), by a matt rather than a shiny surface and by a richness of tone. Especially in Britain cultured taste was drawn particularly to the calotype process, which had the same characteristics as a print, rather than to the highly-polished metal daguerreotype or to the later albumen process on paper, which carried its clearly-detailed image in a film of egg white. The contemporary critic and writer on photography, Thomas Sutton,[15] was obliging enough to nail his colours to the mast in defence of these criteria. *The Liverpool and Manchester Photographic Journal* of 1859 contained the following:

> As a matter of taste, he [Mr Sutton] extremely dislikes prints on albumenised paper, and no doubt there are many who probably entertain the same feelings, and it is for them that the present article is intended. Those who prefer that peculiar kind of vigour and brilliancy which is exhibited by a piece of black sticking plaster, or a well polished Wellington boot, to the depth and vigour of the blacks of a fine engraving on plate paper need not concern themselves with this process; for the best results which it appears capable of yielding do not surpass, in point of vigour, the best proofs from the press of the copper plate.[16]

Thomas Sutton was a prolific writer and contributor to most journals throughout the 1850s and early 1860s. Irritatingly opinionated, simultaneously conservative and radical, he was incapable of acknowledging any merit in work that did not conform to his rigorous ideal. Stephen Thompson[17] forthrightly criticised such a narrow and ungenerous philosophy:

> Art is conservative. We cling to old associations with desperate tenacity; but time softens down many prejudices, dispels many illusions and teaches many wholesome if unpalatable lessons. There are, or were, those who denied photography admission into the palace of Art; who, in its obvious defects could not descry its obvious possibilities.[18]

Wood shared with Sutton a conservative approach to photography in the sense that he continued to use the coarse paper negative after the invention of the glass negative. Like DO Hill and Robert Adamson, he produced photographic prints that were rich and fine in appearance and belong to the centuries-old print-making tradition, as much as to a new and revolutionary art-form.

[26] The mezzotint[19] (fig 6) although originated by Ludwig von Siegen[20] of Amsterdam in 1642, was so widely adopted and practised in England that it became known as the *manière anglais*. It represented a radical departure in that the effect previously achieved by systematic crosshatching of line (fig 7) was replaced by a random granular structure that created an illusion of tone . The characteristics of the mezzotint, aquatint[21] (fig 8) and lithographic print[22] (fig 9) clearly informed contemporary

15 Thomas Sutton (1819-1875) was a prolific writer on photography and was closely associated with the French photographer Louis-Désiré Blanquart-Evrard. See Isabelle Jammes, *Blanquart-Evrard et les Origines de l'Édition Photographique Française, 1851-55*, Geneva, 1981 and Thomas Sutton, 'Reminiscences of an Old Photographer', *Photographic Notes*, 1867, pp 233-235.

16 Article possibly by Blanquart-Evrard on 'Mr Sutton's Developing Process', quoted in Isabelle Jammes, op. cit.

17 According to AJP Arnold, op. cit. p 309, Stephen Thompson was responsible for the images in *Photographs of the Collection in the British Museum*, published in 1872.

18 'Notes on the present Exhibitions', *The Photographic Journal*, 1861, p 110.

19 Mezzotint involves raising a uniformly dark barb or ground on the plate with a toothed tool. The designs are traced upon the plate, and the light parts are gradually scraped off. See *Printing Patents: Abridgements of Patent Specifications relating to printing 1617-1857*, first published 1859, reprinted by the Printing Historical Society, London, 1969.

20 'The inventor of the mezzotint was Ludwig von Siegen, an officer who had been in the service of the Landgrave of Hesse-Cassel. He settled at Amsterdam, and his first plate, executed in 1642, was a portrait of the Landgrave's mother. In 1654, when at Brussels, von Siegen communicated his invention to Prince Rupert, who upon his return to England discussed its merits with John Evelyn, whose "Sculptura" in 1662 contains the first account in English of the new process,' Arthur Haydon, *Chats on Old Prints*, London, 1906.

21 The aquatint is printed from a rough surface bitten by acid through a pitted layer of resin on the metal plate.

22 A planographic process relying on the antipathy of grease to water. The lithograph is printed from a limestone block where acid has bitten round a drawing done in greasy chalk.

opinions of what constituted, aesthetically and perceptually, an acceptable representation. By the middle of the nineteenth century, printmaking had reached such unsurpassed heights of subtlety and rendition of colour, tone and hue, that almost impossible criteria were established and ruthlessly applied to the infant photography. Turner's *Liber Studiorum*[23] had just been published and still stands today as one of the greatest achievements in landscape executed in mezzotint (fig 10).

The evolution of the reproduced image from the woodcut through the engraving, mezzotint, aquatint, and lithographic print to the photograph represents a progression towards a direct form of representation, a reductive process.[24] In the mid 1850s, photographers were still unable to match the subtle control of colour and tone achieved by the print-makers. It was in pursuit of this subtlety that John Muir Wood was to experiment rigorously with the toning methods which gave an effective richness and impact to his own prints.

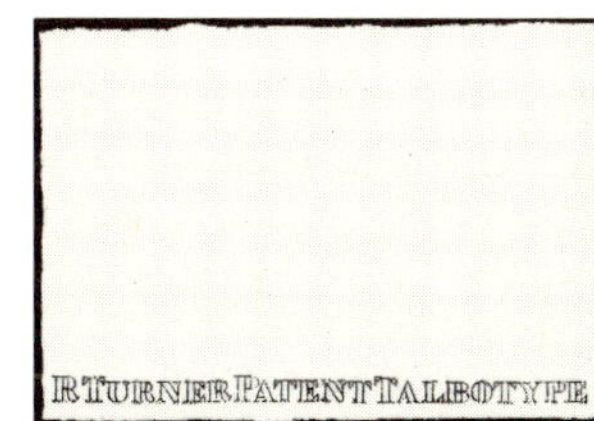

Fig 5 R Turner Patent Talbotype Watermark
photographic base paper about 1852

Image Stability and Permanence: The subsequent control and manipulation of colour by toning with the salts of rare metals

The early photographs were often unattractive in colour and prone to fading. Toning prints served a double purpose of improving the colour and increasing the stability of the print. The most sucessful way of toning proved to be the use of gold, and several of Wood's photographs are annotated with the word 'gold'.

Dr Alfred Donné[25] announced in 1839 a method of etching the daguerreotype with acid which turned the photograph into an intaglio printing plate. Hippolyte Fizeau improved Donné's process in 1842 by plating the highlights with gold, which strengthened and protected the image. This was the first recorded use of gold in photography.[26] With the daguerreotype it was possible to carry out all the toning operations with a sufficiently high degree of control and chemical purity. This was not the case with paper photography and the experiments in this area were at first unsuccessful.

Apart from a publication by PF Mathieu in 1847[27] the next work advocating the use of gold was by Gustav Le Gray between 1850 and 1854.[28] He recommended two combined toning and fixing formulae, the first by adding silver nitrate to sodium thiosulphate and allowing the solution to ripen, and the second, the *sel d'or* bath.

In his 1855 edition of *Photographic Manipulation*,[29] Gustav Le Gray again advocated the use of the combined toning and fixing bath with precise instructions for obtaining specific colours by varying the length of time that the print remained in the solution. Unfortunately, the most likely result of a prolonged immersion in either of these baths would be to subject the print to a secondary toning action, particularly if the gold had become exhausted. Inherently unstable complex sulphur compounds are formed in an exhausted *sel d'or* bath that have the potential to destroy the silver image. A practical study of the degradation of the combined toning and fixing bath was undertaken by T Frederick Hardwich, Lecturer in Photography at King's College, London.[30] Although elements of his work were inaccurate, the observational and deductive skills he brought to bear on the problem enabled him to recommend that the practice should be abandoned immediately.

23 Joseph Mallord William Turner, *Liber Studiorum*, 1807-1819.

24 What seemed revolutionary at the time is now seen as a natural and inevitable progression. Photography became all pervasive: photomechanical and photoreproductive systems eventually evolved to supersede and replace mainstream autographic printmaking methods by the beginning of the twentieth century. See Walter Benjamin, 'The Work of Art in the Age of Mechanical Reproduction', *Illuminations*, translated by Harry Zoln, London, 1973.

25 Dr Alfred Donné, (1801-1878), see Raymond Lécuyer, *Histoire de la Photographie*, Paris, 1945, pp 248 and 323.

26 Fizeau's process was not toning in the accepted sense, but it established the precedent for the use of gold in photography. It was realised that the deposition of gold effectively intensified and improved the contrast and colour of the daguerreotype image. Ibid, pp 36 and 247

27 PF Mathieu, *Auto-Photographie ou Méthode De Reproduction Par la Lumière des Dessins, Lithographies, Gravures, etc., Sans L'Emploi Du Daguerréotype*, Paris, 1847, p 14.

28 Gustav Le Gray, *Traité pratique de photographie sur papier et sur verre*, Paris, 1850. Later editions in 1851 and 1854.

29 *Photographic Manipulation. The waxed paper process of Gustav Le Gray*, London, 1855.

30 Hardwich had already commenced investigative work on the problems of permanence in 1854. See Jerome Harrison, *A History of Photography*, London, 1888.

Alkaline Gold Toning: The achievement of greater permanence and control

Hardwich credits James Waterhouse of Halifax with this discovery,[31] but he was also probably aware of the work of CJ Burnett (see p 10) in Edinburgh. He will be referred to later, as part of the theoretical rationale and practical application of alkaline gold toning may be credited to him.

Hardwich established his reputation in articles and correspondence in the *Photographic Journal, Photographic Notes* and *The Liverpool and Manchester Photographic Journal* between 1853 and 1859, where he was frequently in conflict with Thomas Sutton, who still uncritically advocated the methods of Blanquart-Evrard and Gustav Le Gray. In gold toning the use of the separate, alkaline toning bath was fundamental. The discovery was made public as a direct result of the Prince Consort's encouragement of the London Photographic Society to initiate a study of the problem of fading, in 1855. The committee recommended that gold, in some form or other, should be used in the preparation of pictures, 'although every variety of tint may be obtained without it.'[32] The annotation 'gold after fixation' on plate 55 suggests that Wood was following the committee's recommendations.

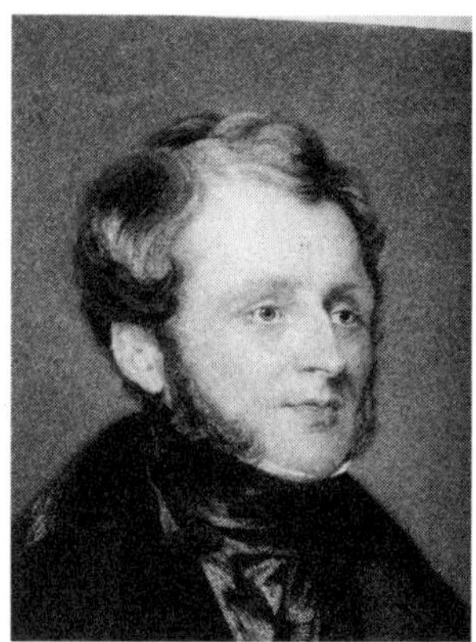

Fig 6 Anon portrait of Lord Edgerton
Mezzotint
private collection

Image Permanence and Toning: the contribution of CJ Burnett

In Scotland in the 1850s, Charles John Burnett was engaged in extensive research into photographic permanence. He wrote a series of succinct and perceptive articles on photographic printing with rare and obscure metals that demonstrate his masterly grasp of the subject.[33] He is worth quoting verbatim because John Muir Wood's knowledge of gold-toning is likely to have been related to his research:

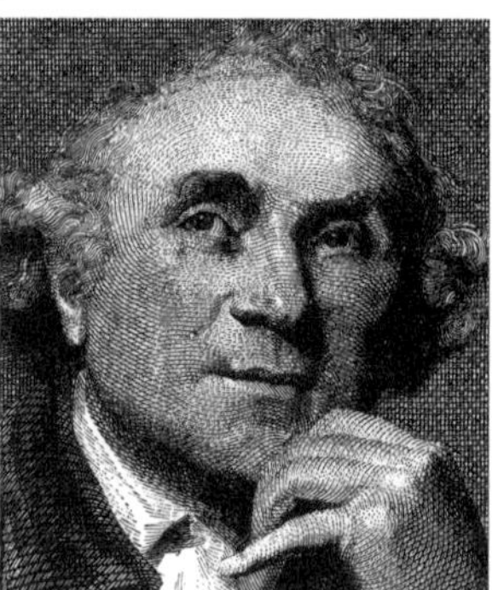

Fig 7 W Sharp from a painting by Reynolds of John Hunter
line engraving
private collection

> Convinced from the first of the error involved in the addition of hydrochloric acid to our ordinary gold bath, and that the move ought rather to be in the opposite direction, it is now * about two years since I recommended to my friends here the use of the alkaline gold bath; the grounds for my recommendation being, that the salt of gold employed is generally the terchloride, containing, as its name implies, three atoms of chlorine to one of gold, and that, consequently, in using a bath of it (chloride of silver consisting of equal atoms of silver and chlorine), for every atom of gold deposited on the print three atoms of silver are lost to the print by being converted to chlorine, necessitating thereby a large amount of overprinting and waste much better avoided, and the evil being further increased if we add acid; while calling in the aid of the alkali or its carbonate (present in the bath either as carbonate or partly in the state of an alkaline aurate, or in combination with auric acid acting as an acid), we remove or diminish greatly this waste, and enable the exchange of the two metals to be conducted in something like terms of fair receprocity. For my statement of its existing in this form I have, I believe, good chemical authority to back me.
>
> (*I have no wish to raise any doubts as to what I see stated as to Mr Waterhouse having independently made use of an alkaline bath; and I am willing to admit his priority, if he used it or recommended it before the summer or spring of 1857. As to the addition of the citrate to the gold bath, that we owe entirely to the accomplished chemist Mr Hardwich.)[34]

31 T Frederick Hardwich, *A Manual of Photographic Chemistry*, London, 1856.

32 *Journal of the Photographic Society*, November 1855, pp 251-252.

33 *The Photographic Journal* published a series of articles by Burnett between April and August 1859, covering experiments with organic acids and rare metals.

34 *The Photographic Journal*, June 1859, p 161.

John Muir Wood's Annotations: the indicators of process and practice

Unlike Burnett, Wood did not write down or publish any research and only a partial idea of his experiments may be gained from the prints themselves. His prints are frequently annotated, but only for personal reference to keep a record of the techniques used in colouration (not yet referred to as toning) and processing. The cryptic nature of the captions makes interpretation and verification difficult, but there are some patterns and constants that emerge.

The following annotations in pencil refer to the use of an ammonia bath and the subsequent toning with copper:

AG 70 co=last (plate 43) That is, seventy grains (4.5 grams) of silver nitrate to a fluid ounce (28 ccs) of distilled water, used after the initial salting and the print was finally toned with copper.

x/w/cl 15 Am Nit (plate 36) An initial wash with sodium chloride (fifteen grains to a fluid ounce) followed by ammonio-nitrate of silver. This is a standard variation of the salt print process in use 1839 to 1855, which was first noted in WHF Talbot's Notebook 'P'.[35]

Am wk co That is, ammonia weak copper, indicating the use of ammonia as a fixing agent before toning with copper.

In the first edition of his *Art of Photography*, published in 1841, Robert Hunt states:

> Chloride of silver being soluble in a solution of ammonia and some of its salts, they have been recommended for fixing agents. The ammonia however attacks the (silver) oxide, which forms the darkened part in some preparations, so rapidly, that there is a risk of destroying the picture, or at least impairing it considerably. It matters not whether the liquid ammonia or its carbonate be used, but it must be a very dilute solution.[36]

If John Muir Wood had used this ammonia bath without washing the print, it would have left it in an ideal alkaline condition for toning with copper.

The use of copper sulphate in conjunction with potassium bromide or iodide was known by the mid 1850s as an intensifier for glass plate negatives but not as a toning agent for prints. No other photographer is yet known to have used copper in this way before the 1890s and it is evidence of Wood's chemical originality or more generally of the inventiveness of his circle, that he was using this metal. Plates 28 and 51 have the characteristic reddish brown of prints developed with silver nitrate, copper chloride and lead acetate baths.

Wood's interest in copper, and in the use of tin as a further toning agent, may have come from discussions with the Cundells. One of Joseph Cundell's prints in Wood's possession (see fig 2, on page 9) was annotated *N5 Sta Ag 40 Ch10 Ag 20*, which may be read as experiment number five(?), stannous chloride, forty grains of silver nitrate to the fluid ounce of distilled water, ten grains to the fluid ounce of distilled water, ten grains of salt to the fluid ounce of water used to remove the free silver and twenty grains of copper chloride to tone the print. Wood's use of tin without copper can be seen in plates 22 and 37, which were probably made in the 1840s. Tin, like copper, is totally unexpected in the context. Wood was not merely trying the metal out but succeeding in producing a good, durable print. The first mention of trials with tin in

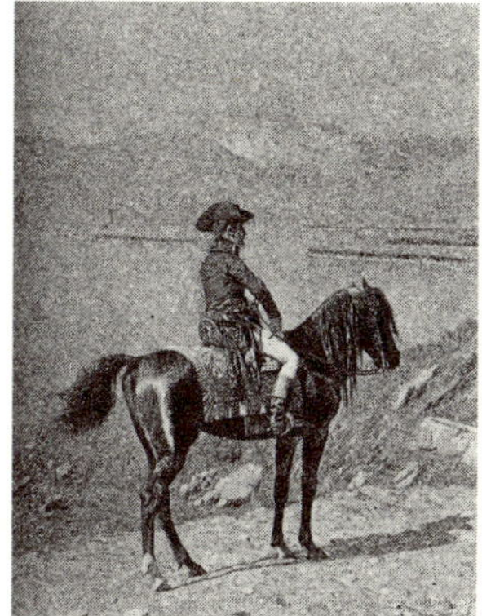

Fig 8 J S Virtue
detail from 'Consulting the Oracle'
aquatint
private collection

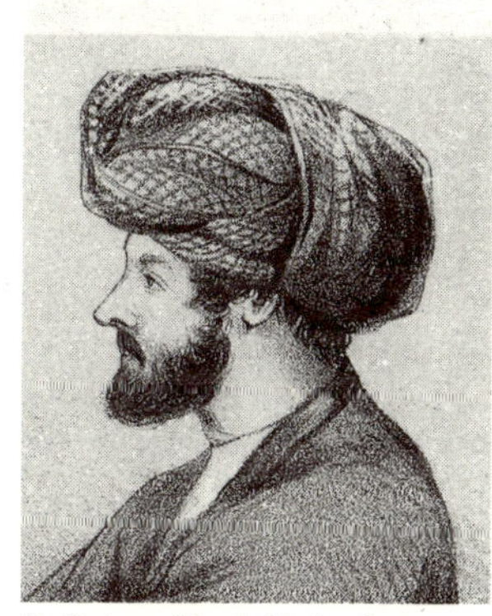

Fig 9 Anon Man in Native Costume
lithographic print
private collection

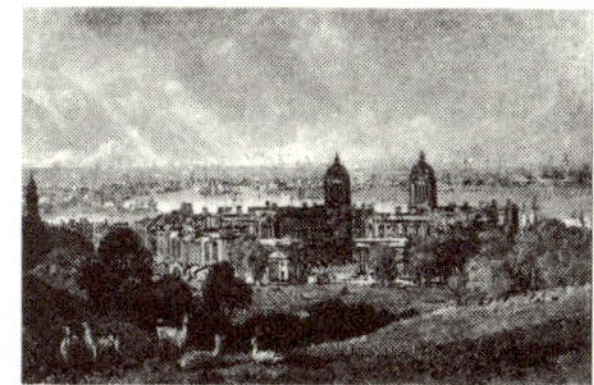

Fig 10 J M W Turner
Mezzotint, Greenwich
Liber Studiorum 1807–1819

35 Science Museum Collection.

36 Robert Hunt, *A Popular Treatise on the Art of Photography*, Glasgow, 1841.

the literature of photography did not appear until the 1880s when it was dismissed as unstable.

In the 1850s, Wood was experimenting with different printing processes. He never abandoned the paper negative of the calotype process for the glass negative albumen process, but he did experiment with albumen, (see plate 18). One of his prints has the inscription, *15 alb + w 50 Ag 2cc*, which may be read as fifteen grains to the fluid ounce of albumen with an equal quantity of water, (this is a comparatively small quantity and there is only a slight glaze on the print), sensitised with fifty grains of silver nitrate in two cubic centimetres of distilled water. This print was probably float coated by laying the paper on the surface of the chemical liquids as the silver solutions that were applied with a Buckle Brush[37] were generally stronger.

The annotation quoted above is written on one of the photographs taken in Bruges in 1847 and is conceivably a remarkably early use of albumen to enhance the detail of the image, but it is more likely to be a later experiment using an old negative. Wood may have learnt the idea of flotation from GS Cundell, who was advocating it in 1844. He was certainly using it the the 1850s. His negative of Melrose Abbey (plate 19) shows a distinct marbling effect (figs 13 and 14) which was caused by the partial oxidisation of the developing agent, the gallic acid bath, which left a film of contamination on the surface.

Wood also experimented with the carbon process in the 1850s. The prints are not annotated but are highly distinctive (plate 34). This was the first successful permanent process which used carbon in a relief layer of gelatine on the paper, rather than the unstable silver. Wood's carbon prints which he made directly from calotype negatives (plate 27), were made well before the process was perfected and marketed in 1864. They have the notable faults of the early trials — insensitivity to the middle tones and a tendency to flake off the paper in the highlights where the layer of gelatine is at its thinnest.

Annotations on other prints provide the clue to a further and more extraordinary process which Wood used with great success. The note, *10 Ag 52 2U*, appears on a photograph which has faded to an unexpected pinkish colour. It may be interpreted as ten grains, probably of sodium chloride, to one fluid ounce of water (or ten parts of a solution of the chloride to ninety parts of water), fifty-two grains of silver nitrate to one fluid ounce of distilled water. The *2U* could refer to two parts of a saturated solution of uranium nitrate to eight parts of water.

Wood's interest in gold toning and the carbon process suggest an association with CJ Burnett who was experimenting with both. Burnett discovered a new process, uranium printing, in 1855 and exhibited prints in Glasgow in the same year. He read a paper on 'Photographic Researches' at the British Association meeting on this occasion and Wood almost certainly attended his talk. Uranium prints were characteristically either a chocolate brown tint or, if gold-toned, of 'a purple inky tint.'[38] The purple inky tint is the colour of Wood's most unusual photographs — ones that cannot be reconciled with the standard calotype process (plate 23) and it is likely that these are uranium prints.

37 A small piece of disposable cotton wool, drawn through the end of a glass tube to form a brush for applying the sensitive solutions to the prepared papers.

38 *A Dictionary of Photography*, edited by Thomas Sutton & George Dawson, London, 1867, p 363.

The Uranium Prints

John Muir Wood's three most remarkable photographs have a chromatic intensity and vibrancy of colour that knows no parallel (plates 11, 23 and front cover). The untrimmed horizontal print of the Groene Rei, in Bruges, taken in 1847 (plate 11) and printed from a calotype negative some ten years or so later, is the result of a combination process based on the salts of uranium.[39] It is either a Cuprotype or Uranium print, developed firstly in ferrous sulphate, ferric chloride and lead acetate baths or possibly in a silver nitrate bath followed by a 1 to 500 solution of auric chloride, with the action being arrested in the former by a weak bath of hydrochloric or acetic acid (without washing). There is a characteristic intensification of the image as a consequence. The woodland study (plate 23) has a much softer quality and has deteriorated along the edges but has the same distinct acid smell[40] as the print of the Groene Rei. The third photograph, the 'Citadel of Namur', (front cover), falls somewhere between the other two in coloration showing a clear separation of tones in the shadow areas.

It is a measure of Wood's enthusiasm for printmaking as well as of his inventive and experimental approach to photography that the relationship between these negatives and their prints not only spanned a large interval of time, but also formed an unfamiliar crosslink between the calotype and uranium processes, just as his carbon prints make an unexpected connection between the calotype and the carbon process.

Unpredictability is the predominant characteristic of the successful amateur, conversely predictability characterises the professional. With the former the degree of commitment to a goal can rarely be gauged. It is this element in the make up of John Muir Wood that provides the stimulus and activates in the onlooker, some 125 years later, a perceptual shift, requiring an adjustment to visual syntax.

The uranium based prints stand as an appropriate climax and postscript to John Muir Wood's work. They bear witness to Wood's skill and inventiveness and represent an important aspect of a complex individual whose personal vision informs and expands our knowledge and understanding of the Scottish photographic tradition.

39 Described in PC Duchochois, *Photographic Reproduction Processes*, London, 1880, p 119, 'the proofs undergo the following gradations in colour, red, reddish-violet, blue-violet black and greenish black' and 'the most beautiful purple violet is obtained'.

40 In the last stage of the uranium process the image is fixed after toning in a weak (usually acetic) acid bath.

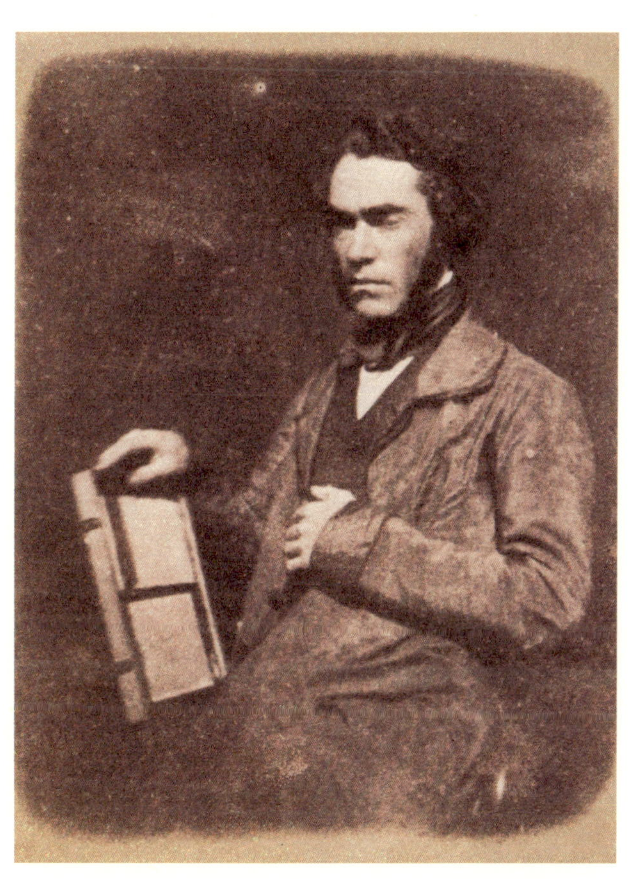

1 **John Muir Wood, holding a photographic printing frame**
salt paper print from a calotype negative
'Br 4'
110 × 80 mm
PGP-W3

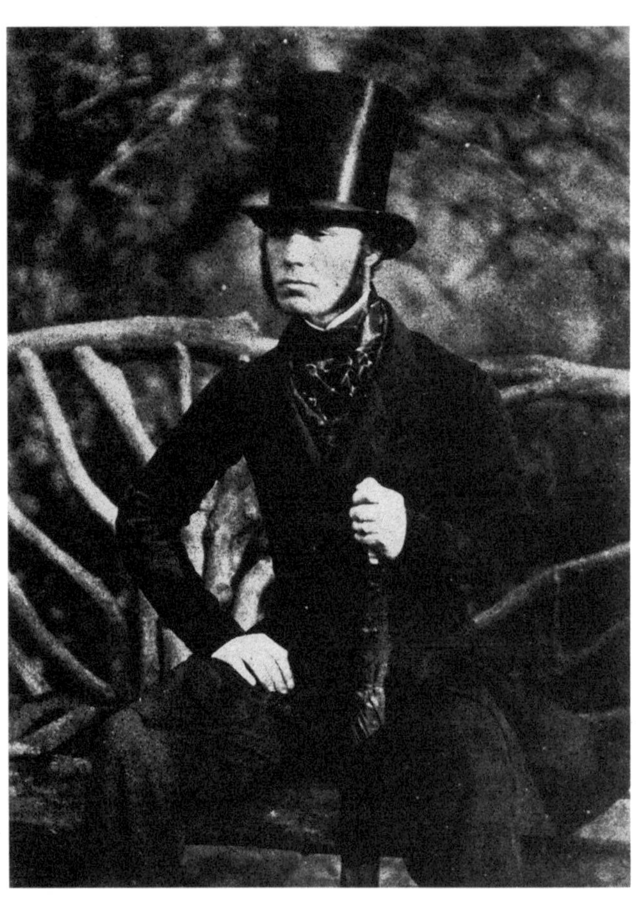

2 **George Wood, John Muir Wood's brother and business partner**
salt paper print from a calotype negative
114 x 83 mm
PGP-W46

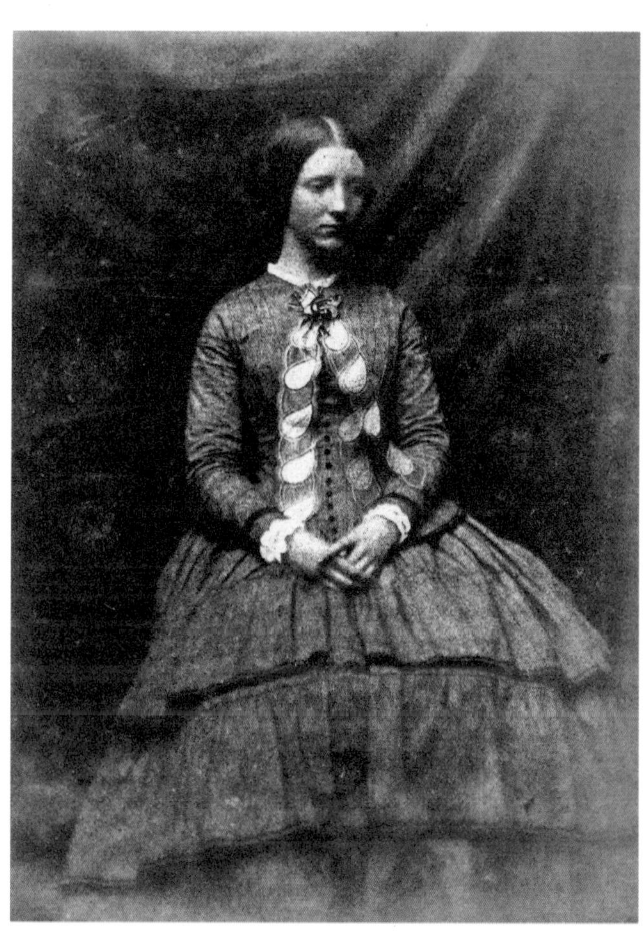

3 **Helen Kemlo Stephen, Mrs John Muir Wood, about 1850**
salt paper print from a calotype negative
133 × 94 mm
PGP-W53

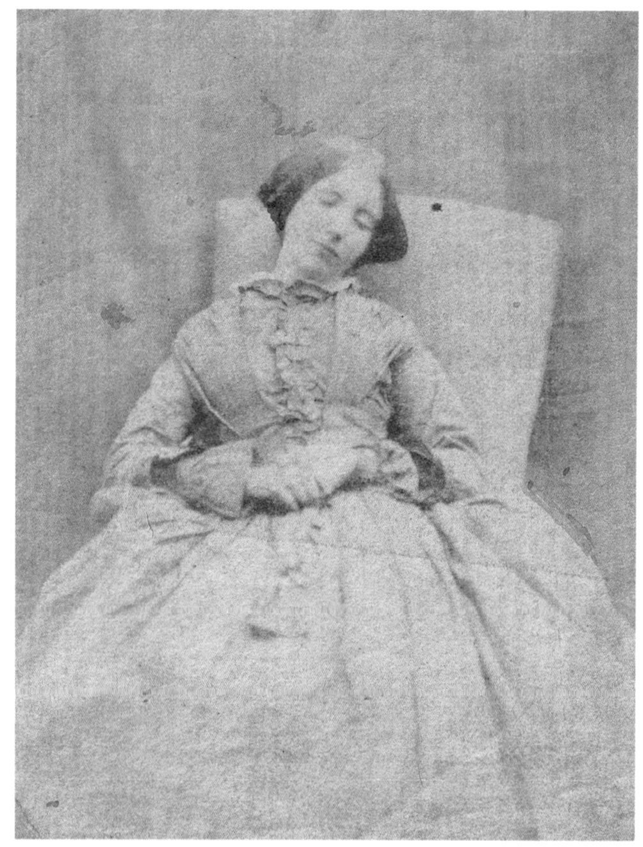

4 **Helen Kemlo Stephen, Mrs John Muir Wood, about 1855**
salt paper print from a calotype negative
122 × 90 mm
PGP-W52

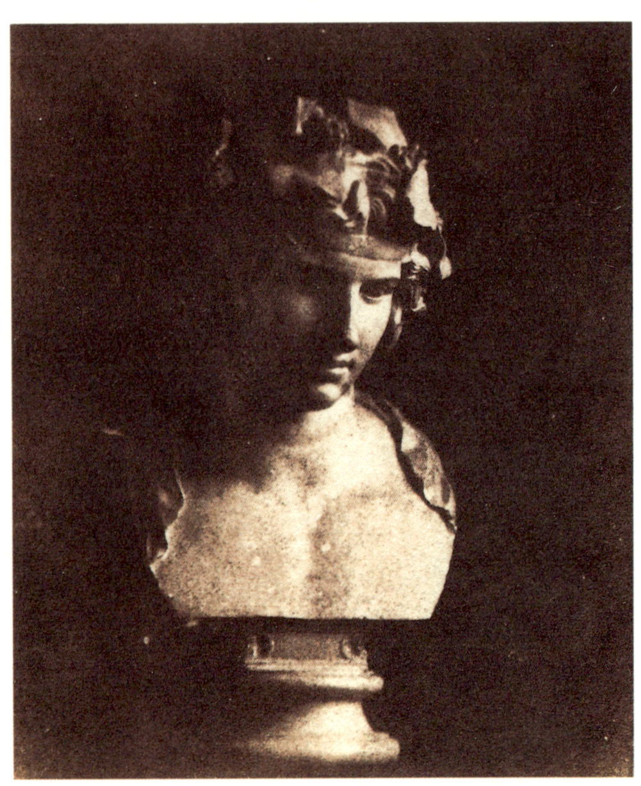

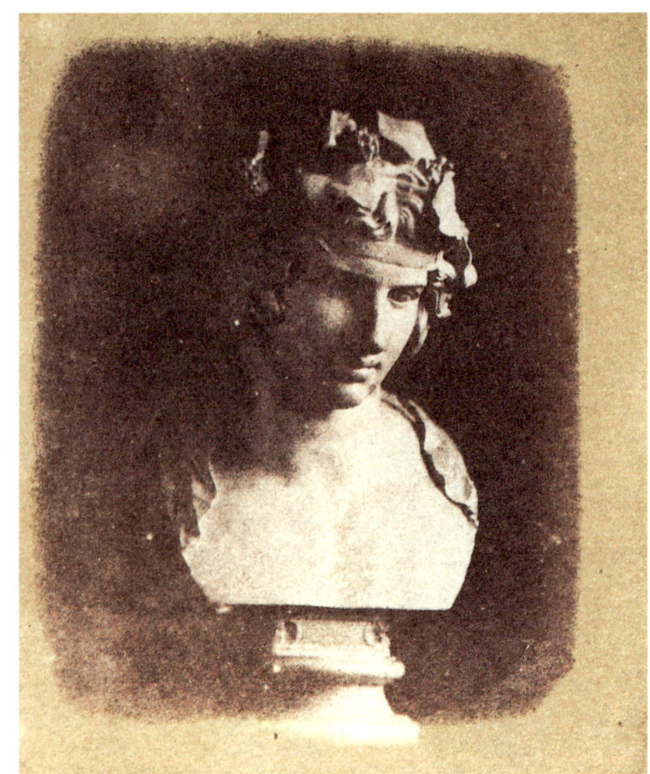

5 **Bust of Bacchus, used to experiment with lighting and toning prints**
toned salt paper print from a calotype negative
118 × 97 mm
PGP-W81

6 **Bust of Bacchus**
toned salt paper print from a calotype negative
'10 B6 Sta B2'
113 × 92 mm
PGP-W82

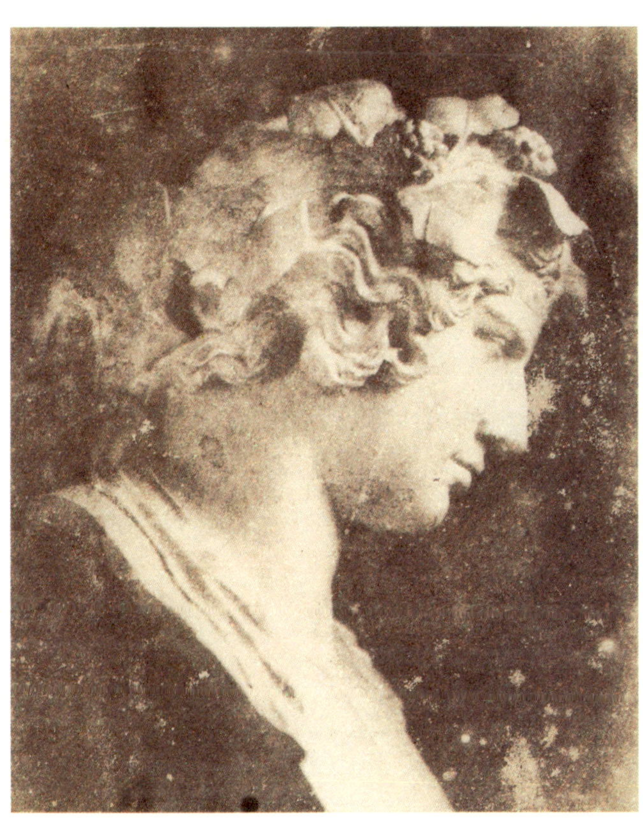

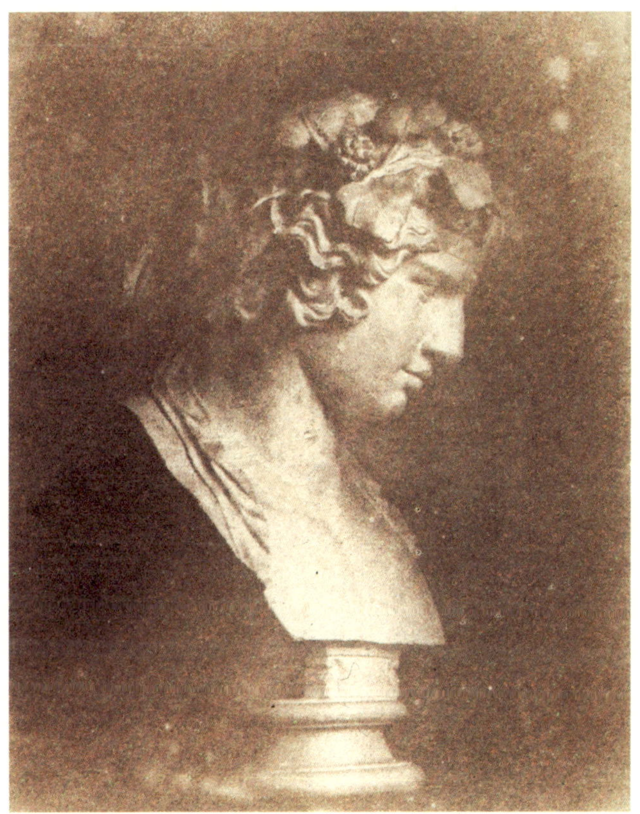

7 **Bust of Bacchus**
toned salt paper print from a calotype negative
'N B A'
129 × 100 mm
PGP-W80

8 **Bust of Bacchus**
toned salt paper print from a calotype negative
'S2 S2'
130 × 100 mm
PGP-W79

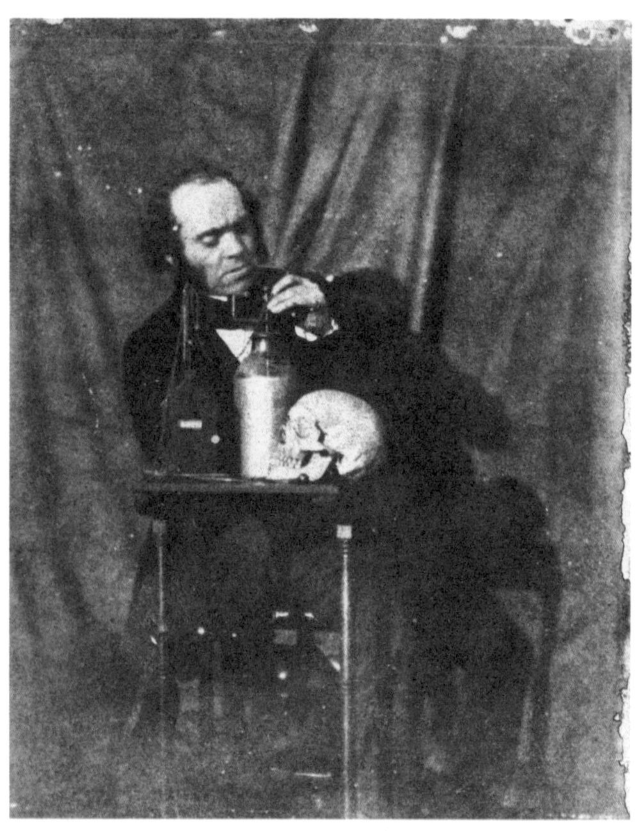

9 **Dr James Jasper MacAldin, flourished 1828-1877, eye surgeon, photographed with an electrical 'thunder house'**
salt paper print from a calotype negative
'Sh Sug'
106 × 83 mm
PGP-W35

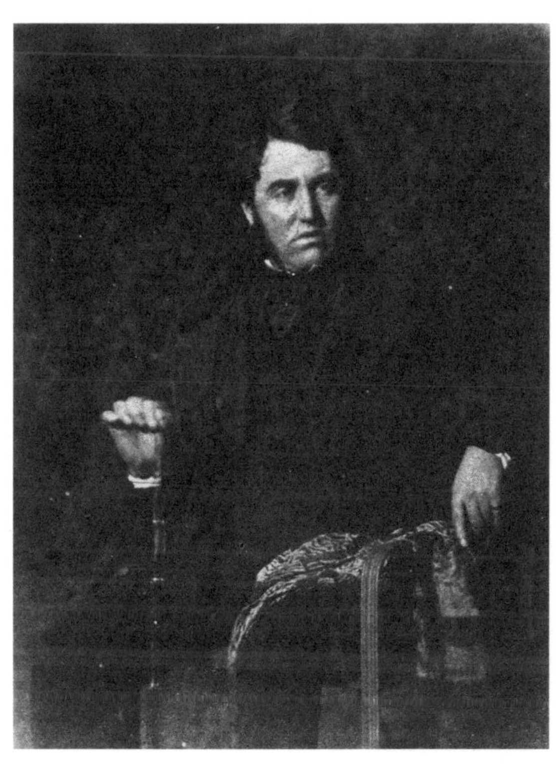

10 **Rev Robert Inglis, Church of Scotland minister at Craigie**
salt paper print from a calotype negative
'Sh[*or* u]Sug'
paper, 'J WHA[TMAN TURKEY MILL] 18[ ]'
PGP-W23

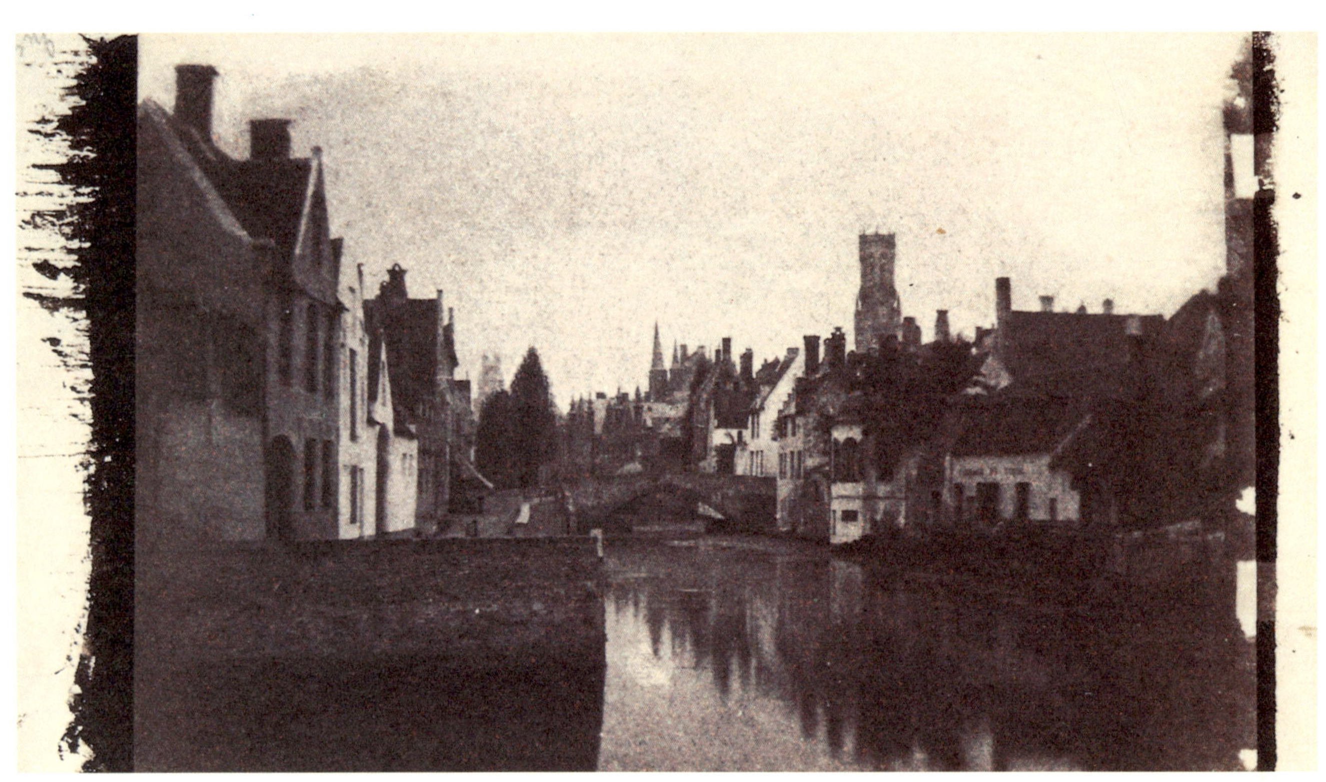

 11 **Bruges, Groene Rei, July 1847**
gold-toned uranium print from a calotype negative
104 × 183 mm
PGP-W62

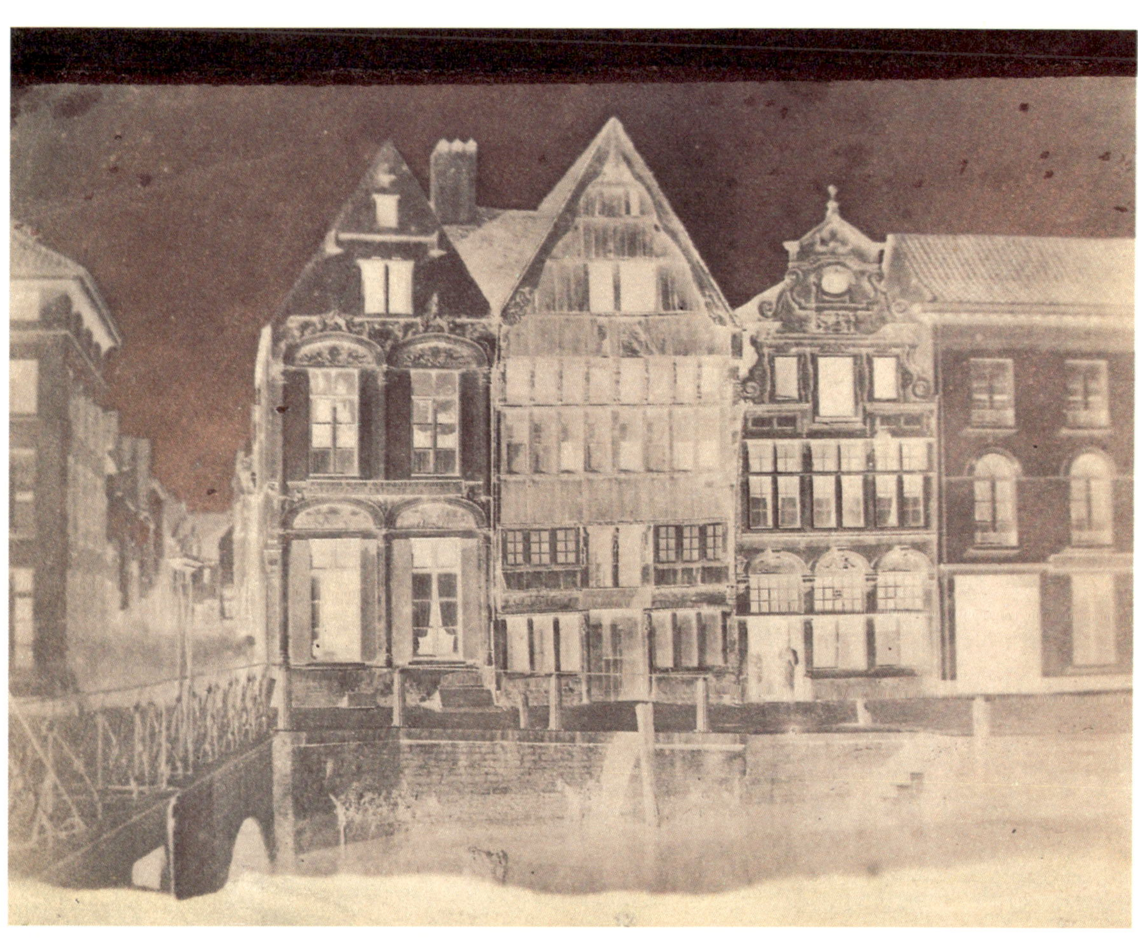

12 **Mechelen, Haverkaai, 2 August 1847**
calotype negative, 'Charles Barry's process', which Wood thought 'sharp but bad in colour & would not print out well'
painted strip added to top edge
119 × 150 mm
PGP-W56

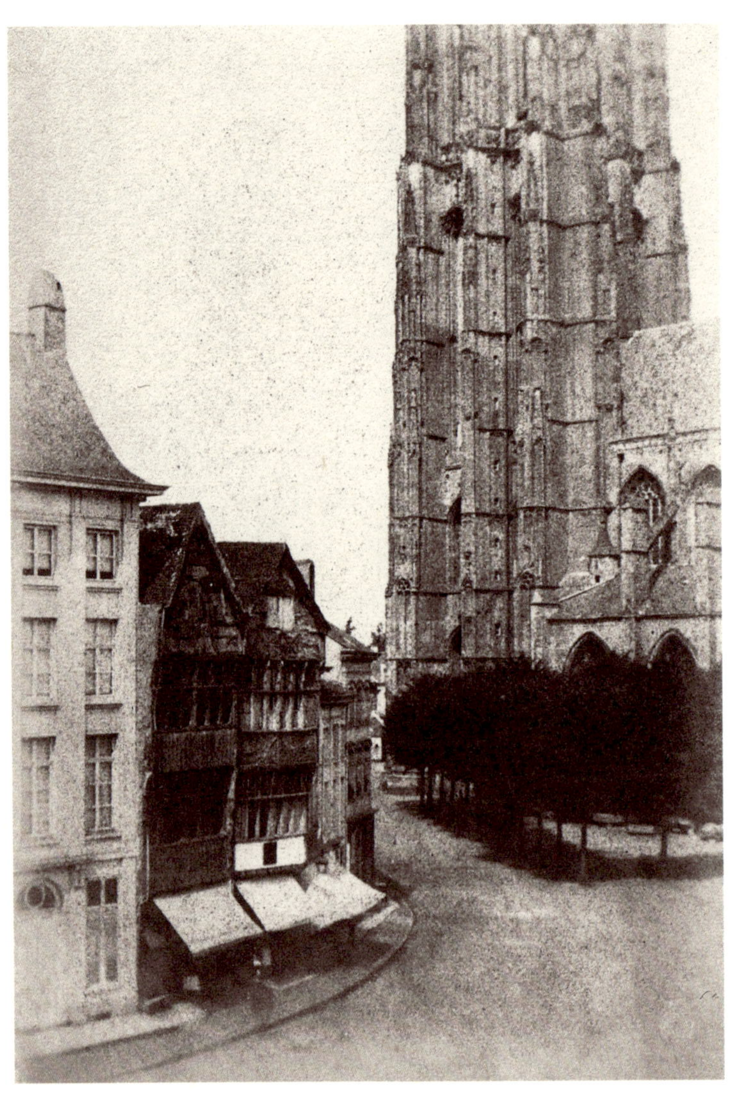

13 **St Romboutskerk, Mechelen, 2 August 1847**
salt paper print from a calotype negative
? Charles Barry's process
140 × 95 mm
PGP-W74

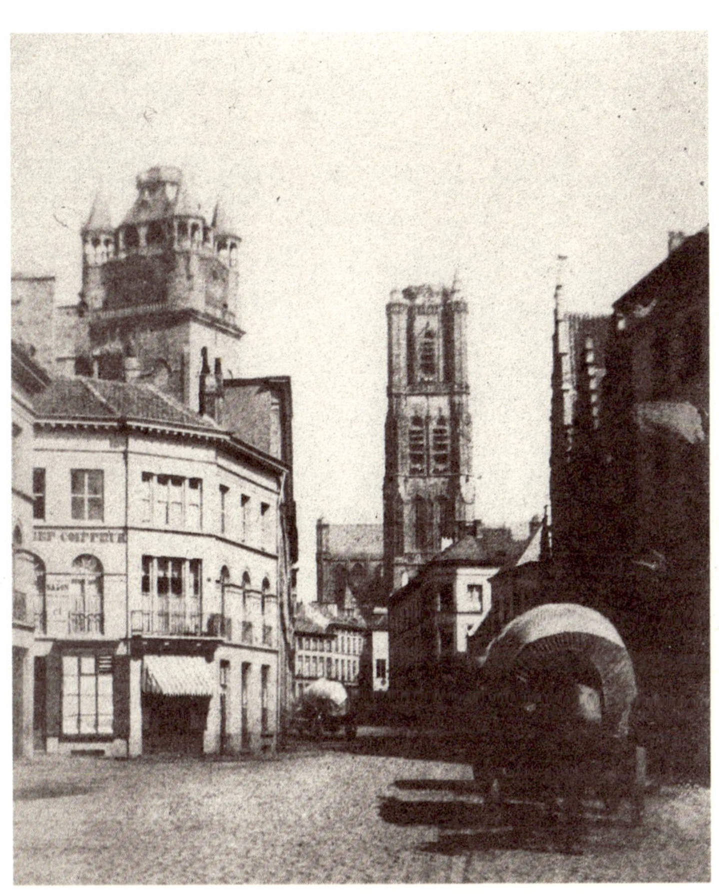

14 **St Baaf's Cathedral, Ghent, 30 or 31 July 1847**
salt paper print from a calotype negative
'W'
113 x 93 mm
PGP-W75

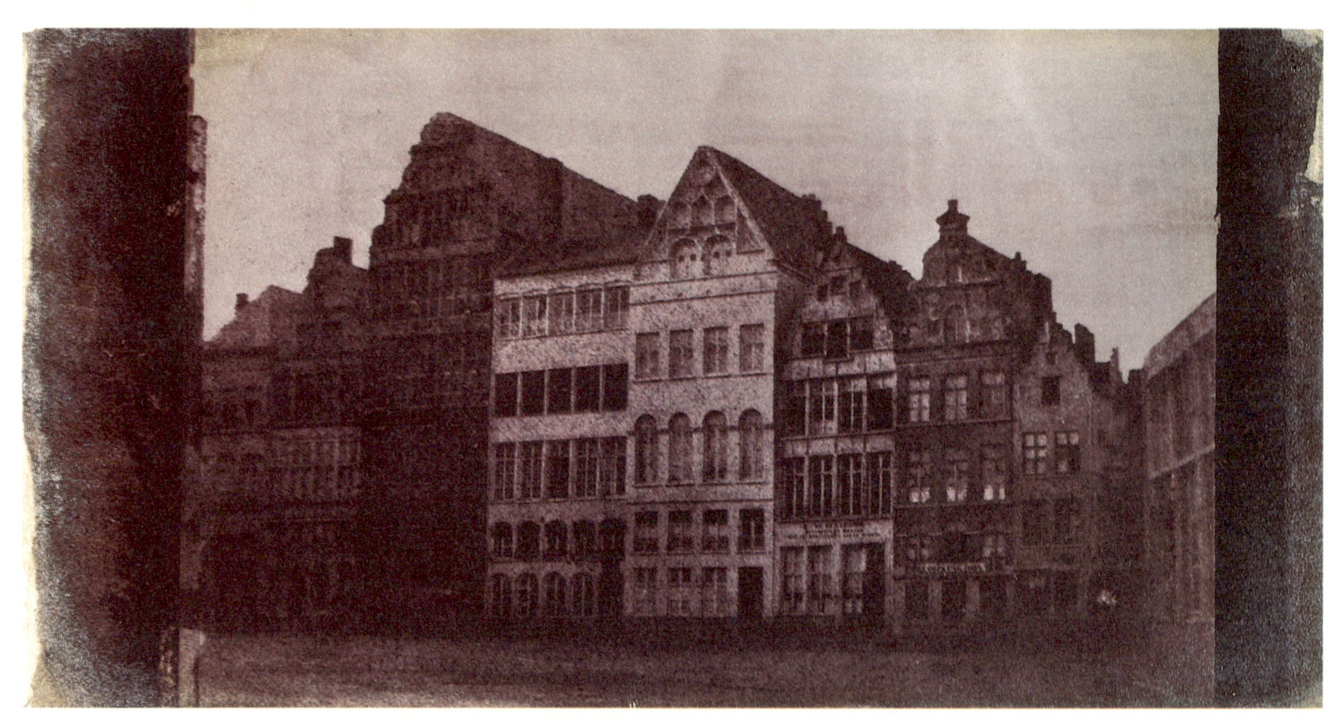

 15 **Antwerp, Guildhalls in the market place, 1847(?)**
gold-toned uranium print from a calotype negative
paper, 'R TU[RNER] CHAFFORD [MILLS]'
103 × 198 mm
PGP-463
PGP-W63

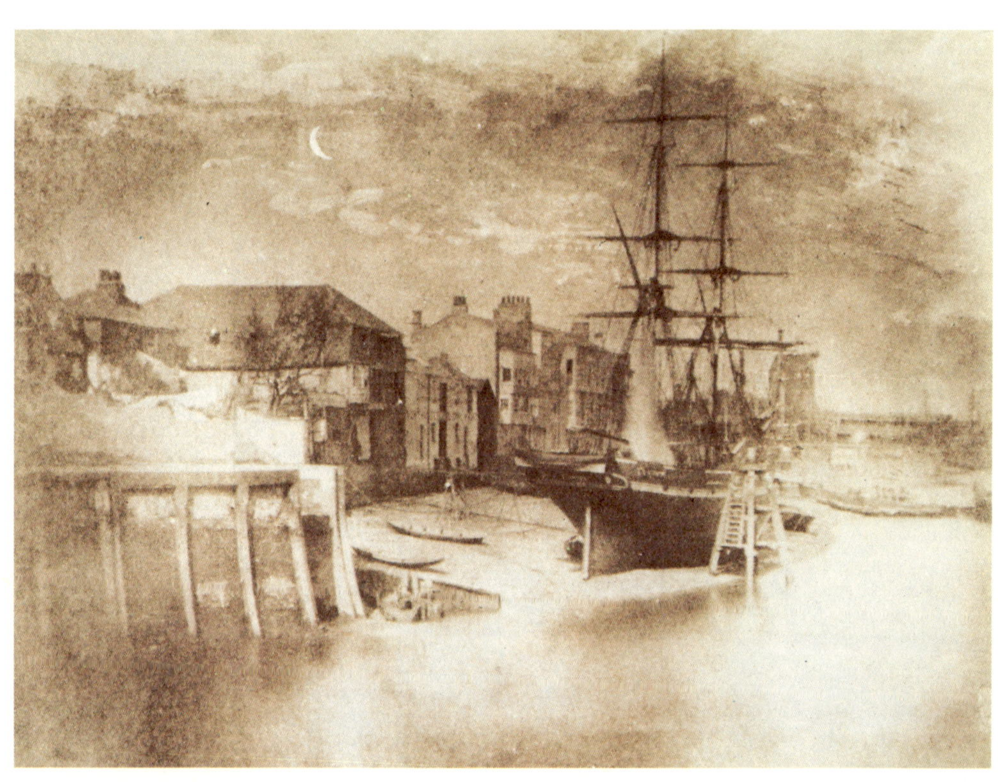

16 **River scene, perhaps the Thames**
salt paper print from a calotype negative, moon and clouds drawn in on the negative
paper, '[WH]ATMAN [TURKE]Y MILL [18]45'
98 × 130 mm
PGP-W86

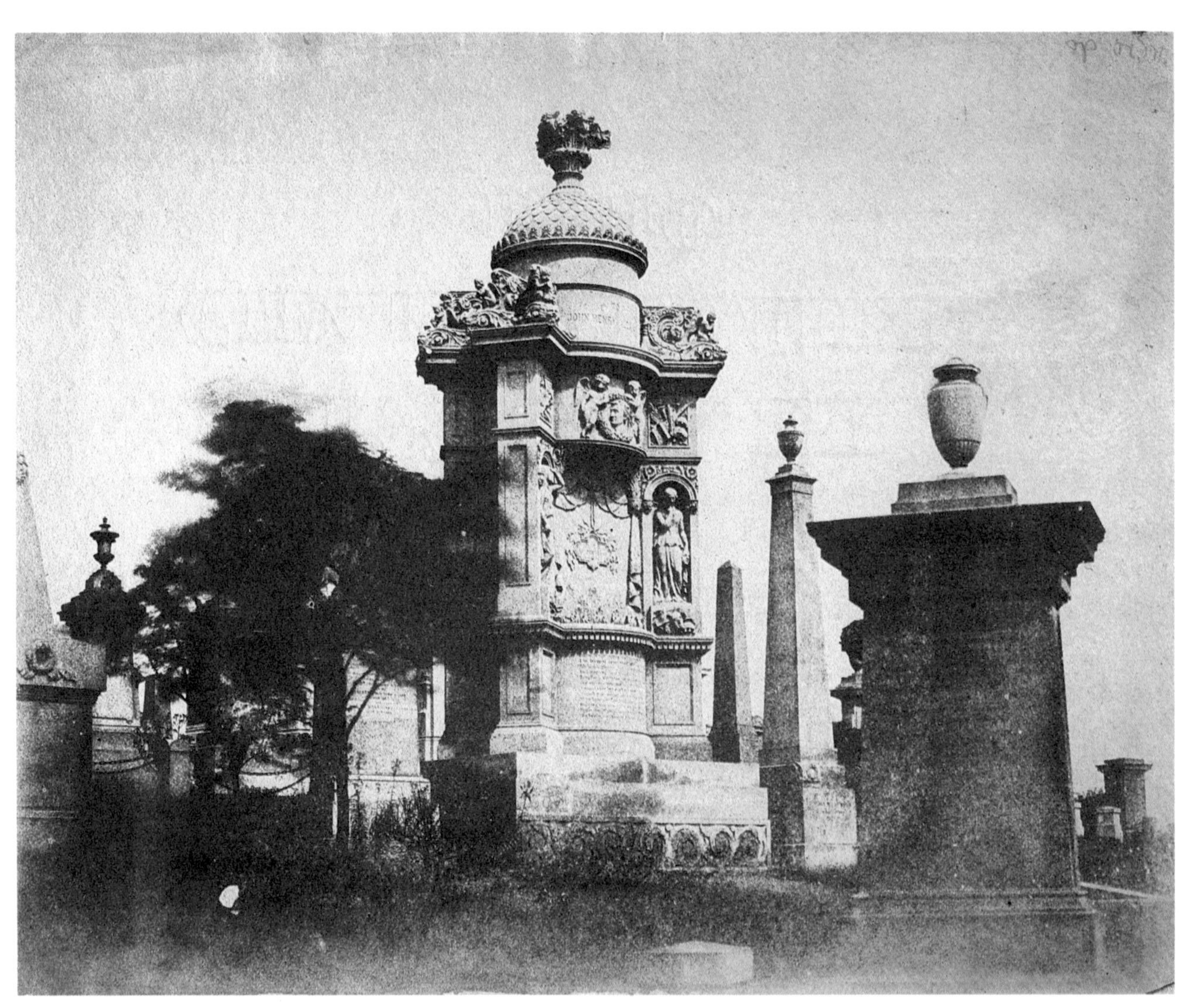

17 **Monument in the Glasgow Necropolis to John Henry Alexander (d 1851), designed by Alexander Handyside Ritchie**
albumenised salt paper print from a calotype negative,
'Ag 20 Clo'
paper, 'R TURNER CHAFFORD MILLS 1840'
188 × 231 mm
PGP-W64

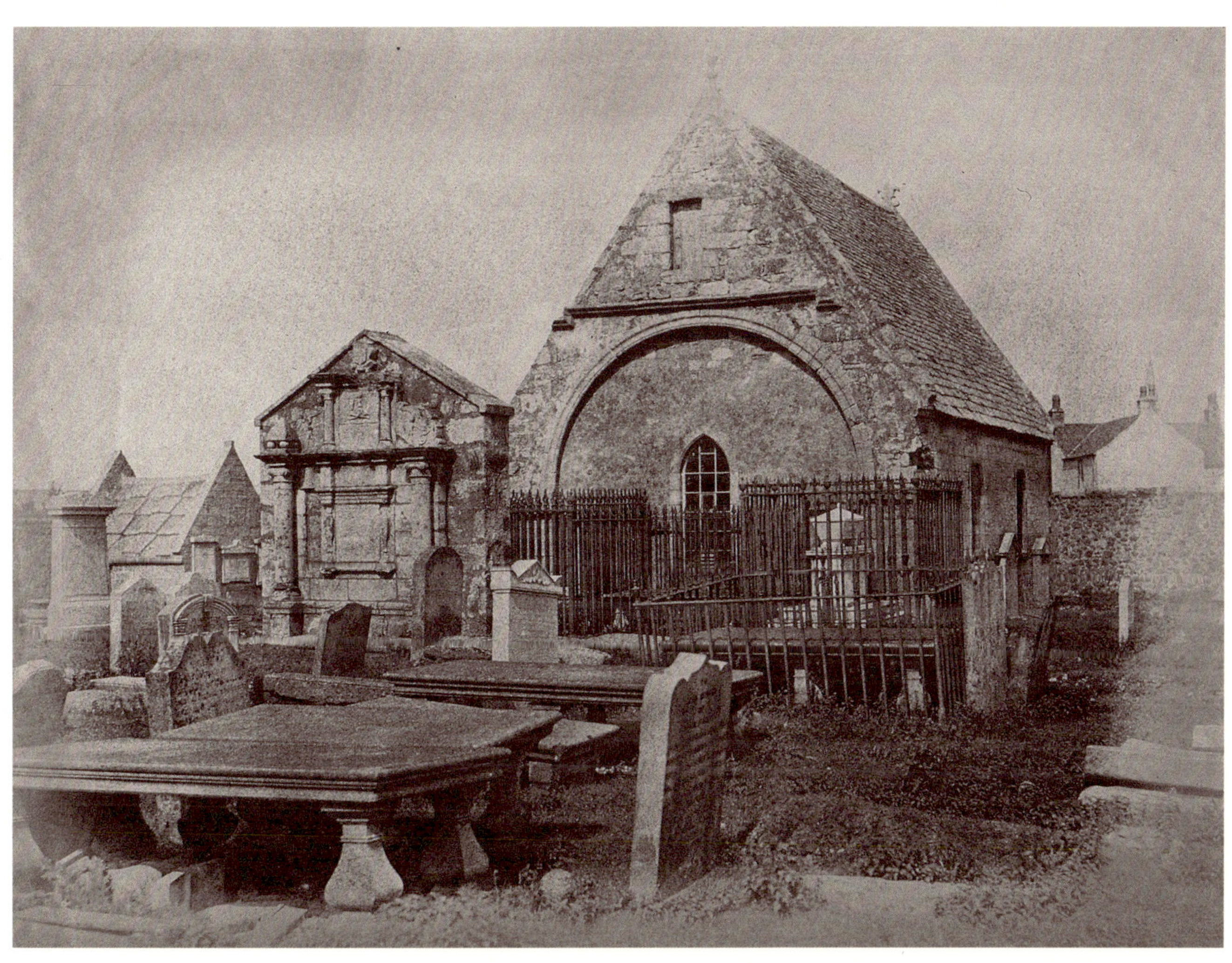

18 **Largs churchyard**
albumenised salt print from a calotype negative
200 × 265 mm
PGP-W66

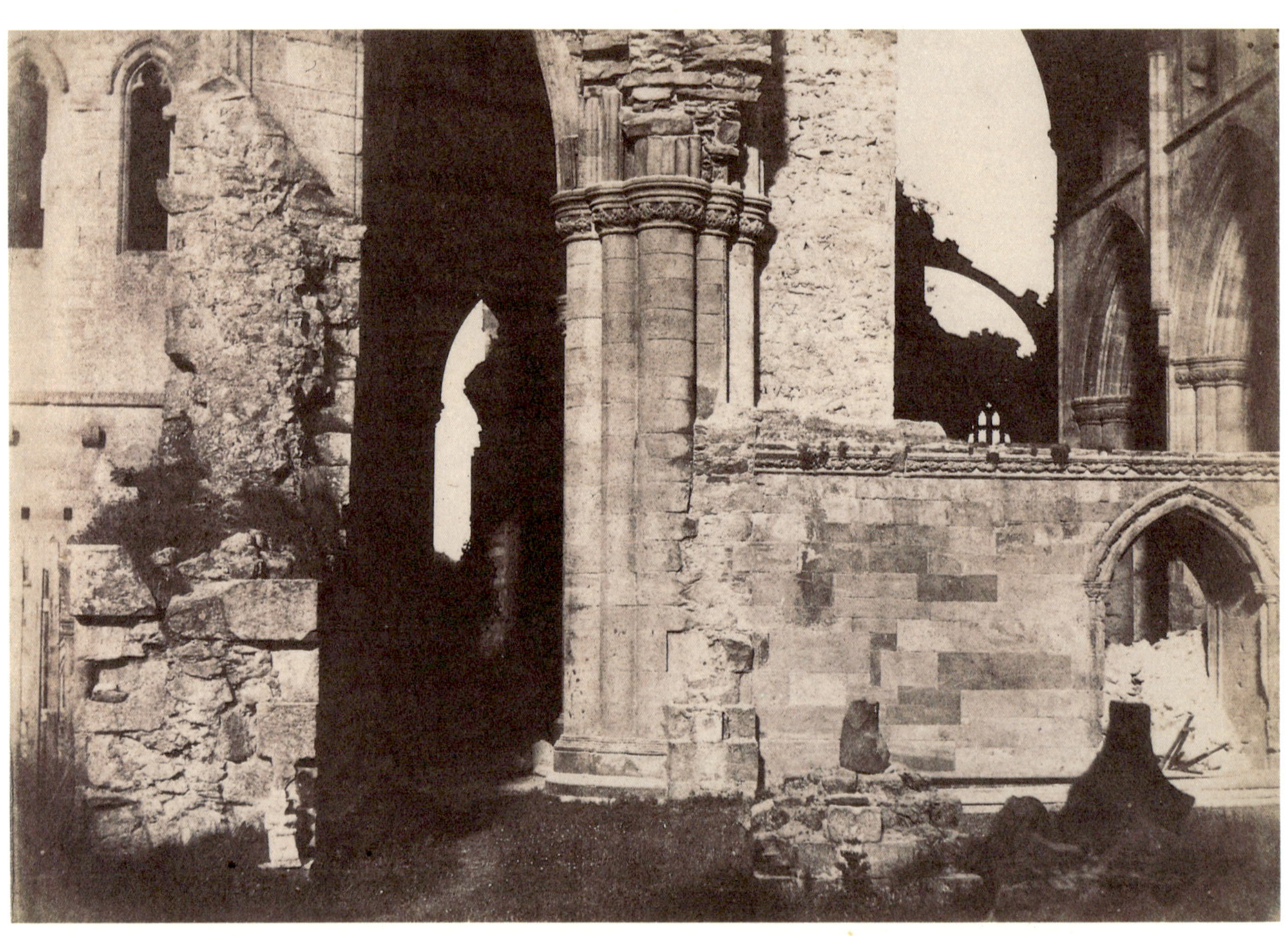

19 **Melrose Abbey**
salt paper print from a calotype negative
157 × 215 mm
PGP-W68

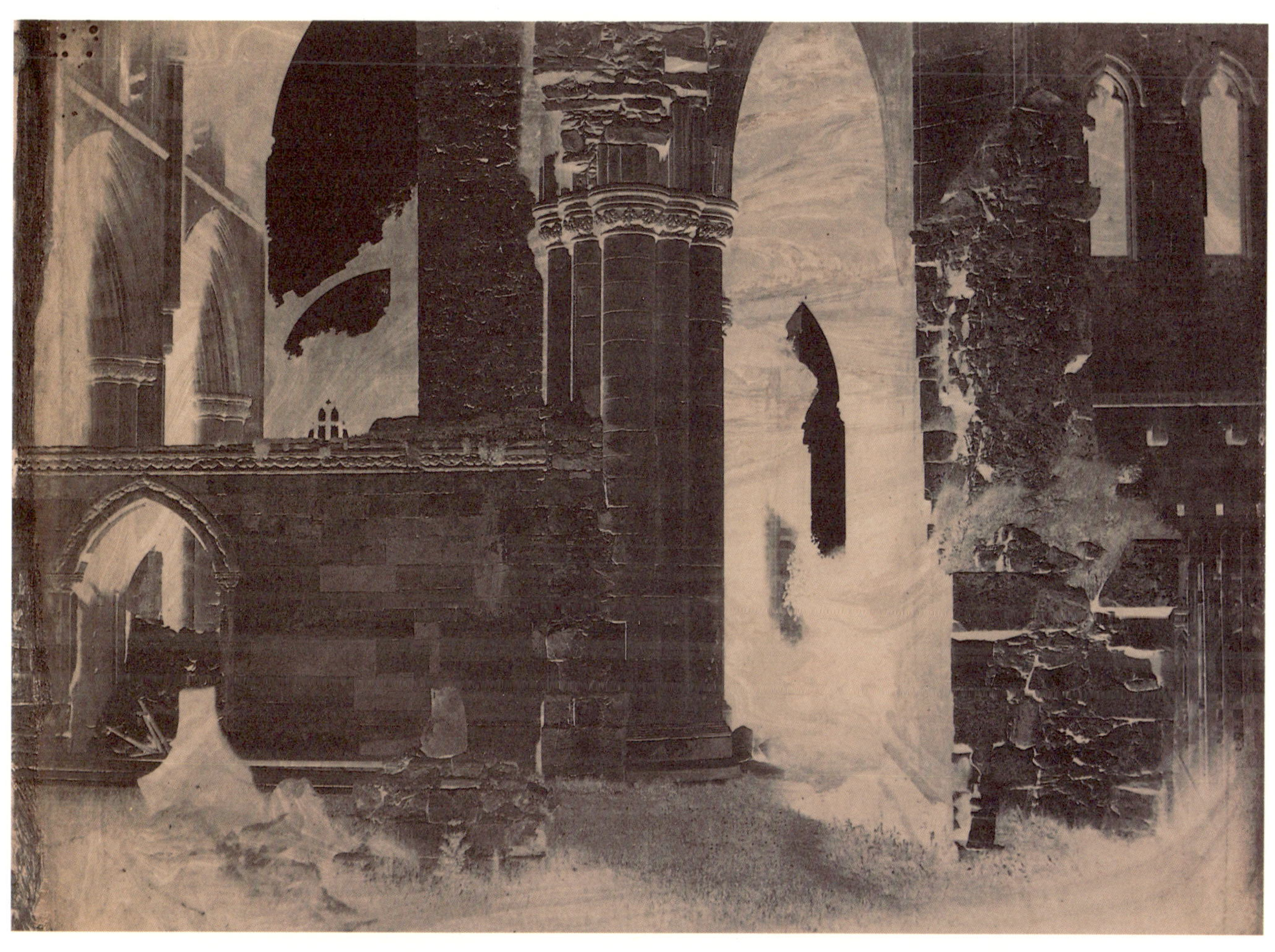

20 **Melrose Abbey**
calotype negative
162 × 232 mm
PGP-W67

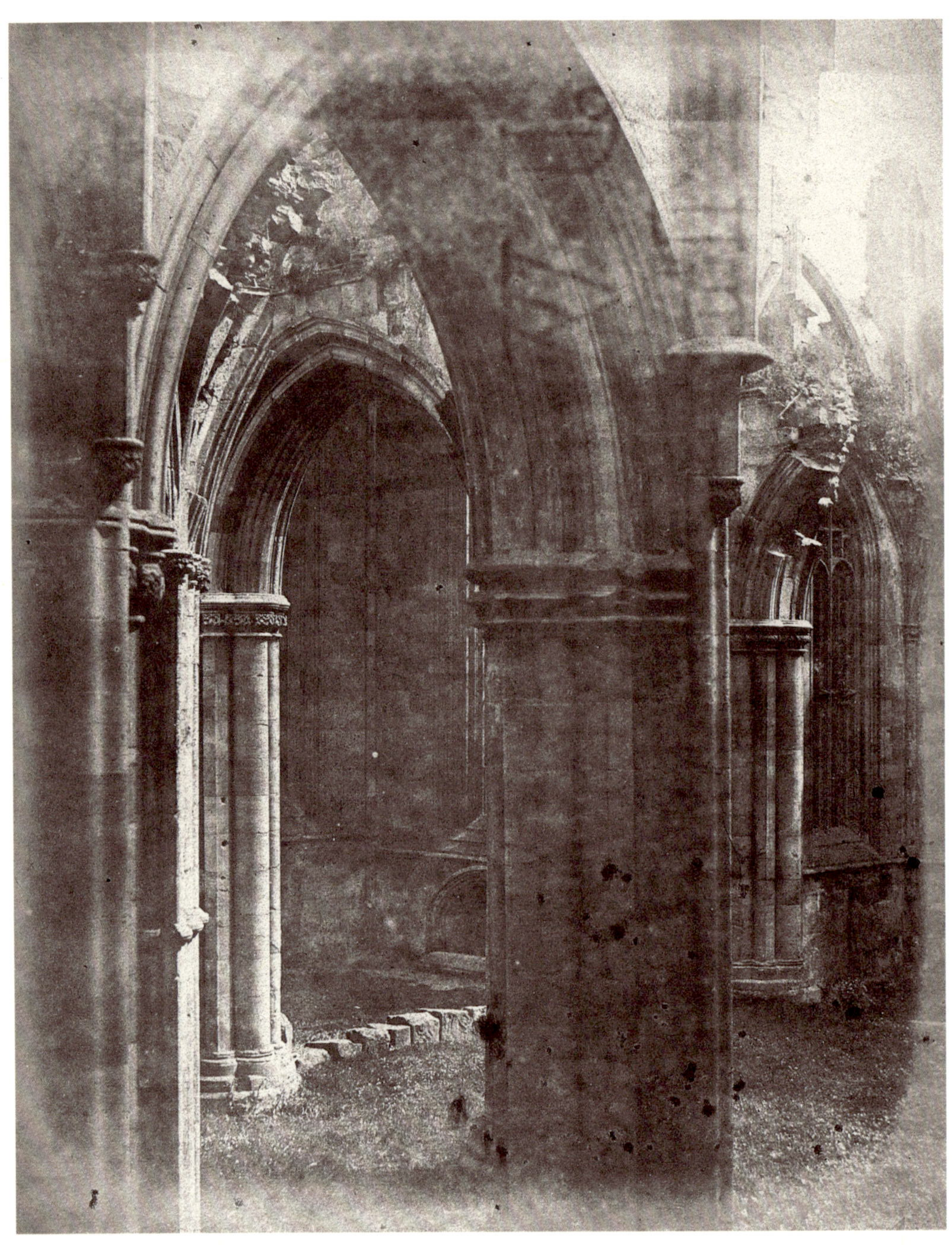

21 **Melrose Abbey**
salt paper print from a calotype negative
paper, 'J WHATMAN TURKEY MILL 1845'
225 × 175 mm
PGP-W69

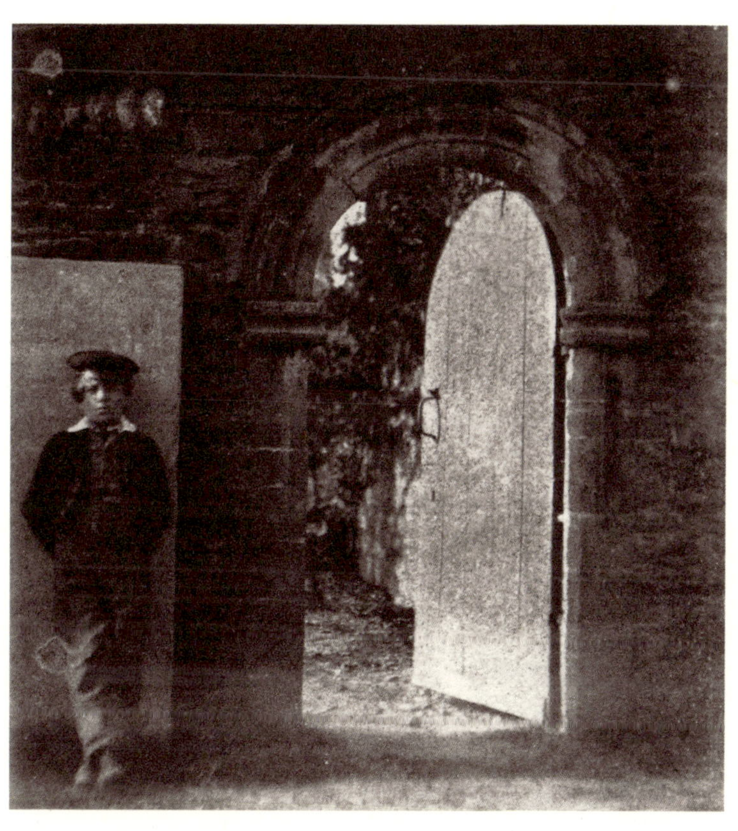

22 **Boy and doorway**
toned salt paper print from a calotype negative
'Sta / Stu B2'
104 × 95 mm
PGP-W91

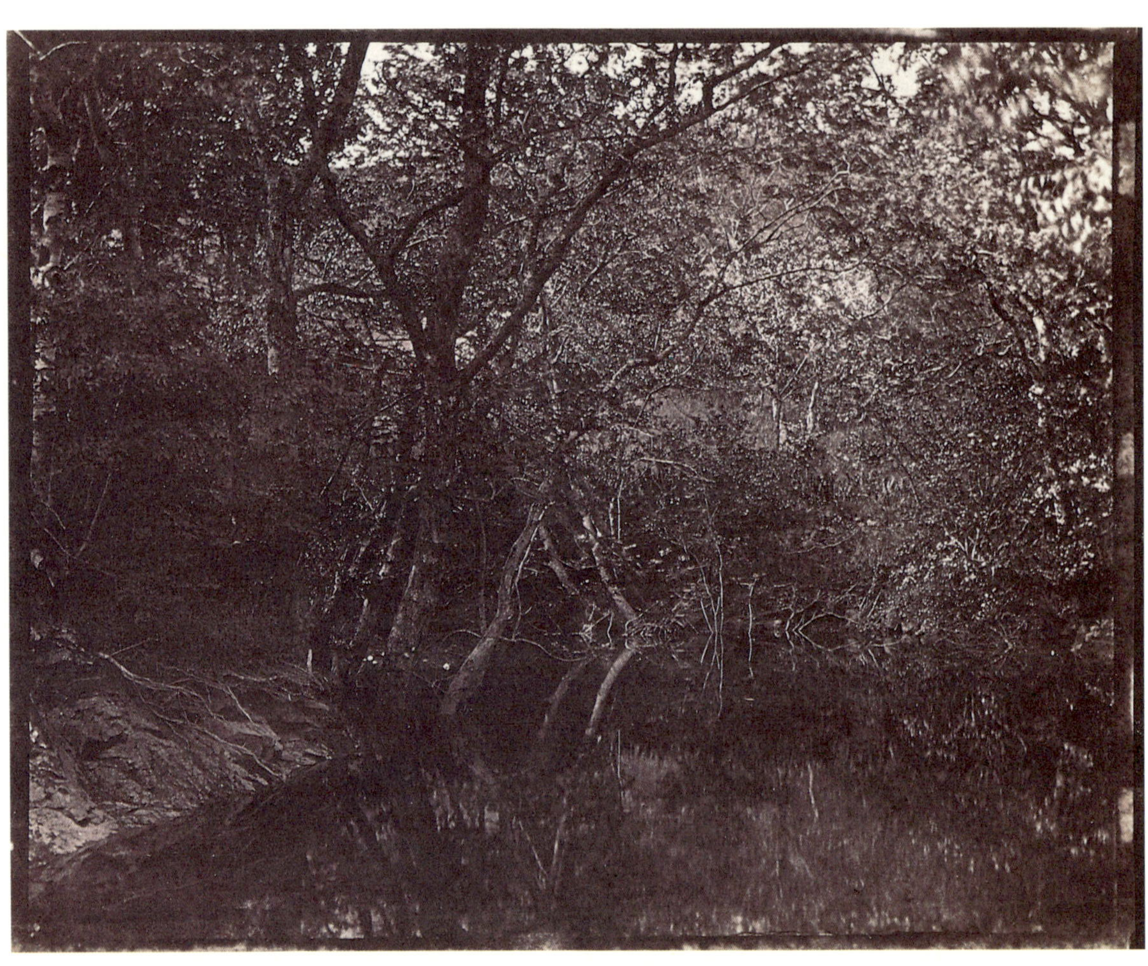

23 **Near Brisbane**
salt paper print from a calotype negative
132 × 202 mm
PGP-W107

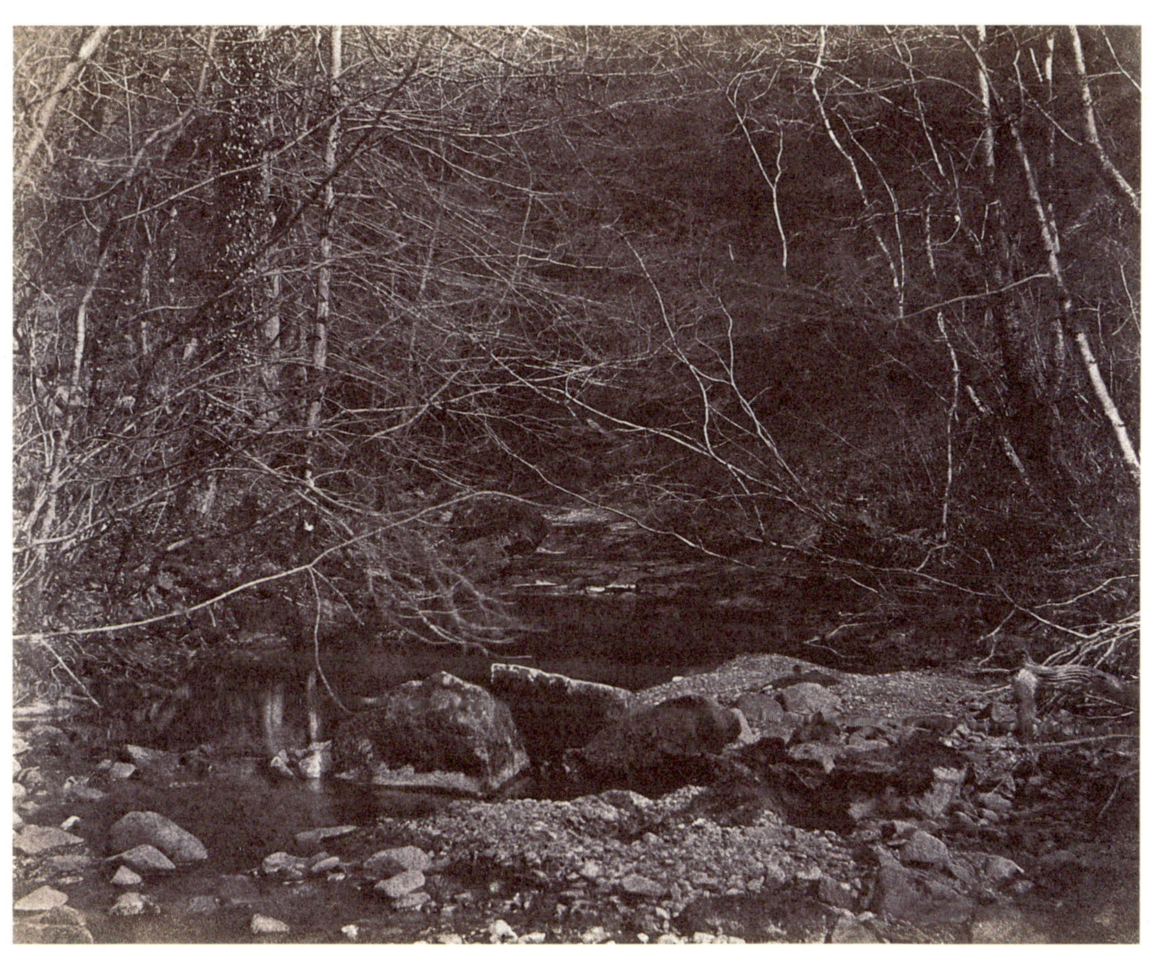

24 **Woodland study**
gold-toned uranium print from a calotype negative
122 × 151 mm
PGP-W96

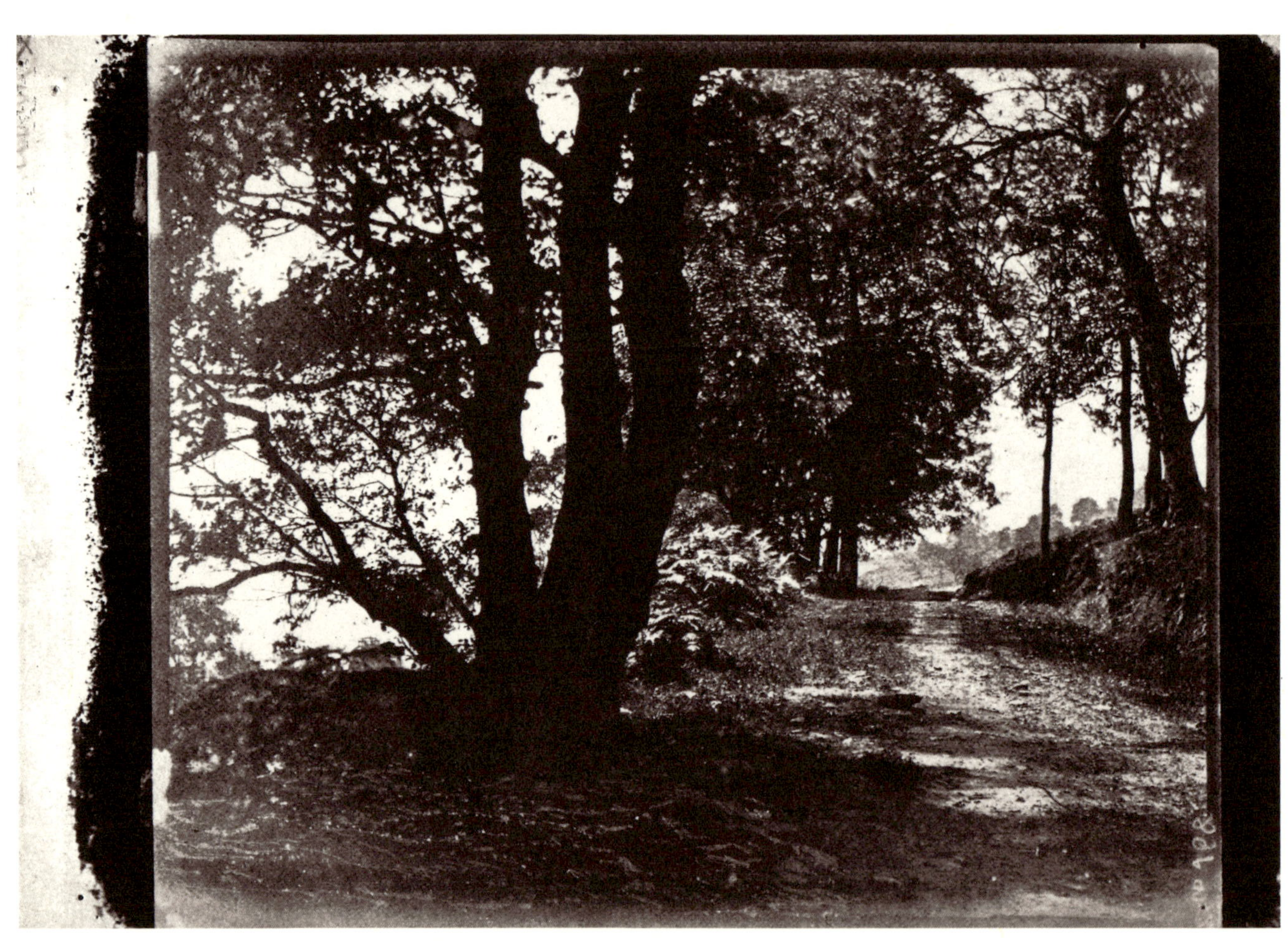

[54] 25 **Tighnabruich**
salt paper print from a calotype negative
'clo wk x'. '[ ]168' printed off from negative
135 × 190 mm
PGP-W108

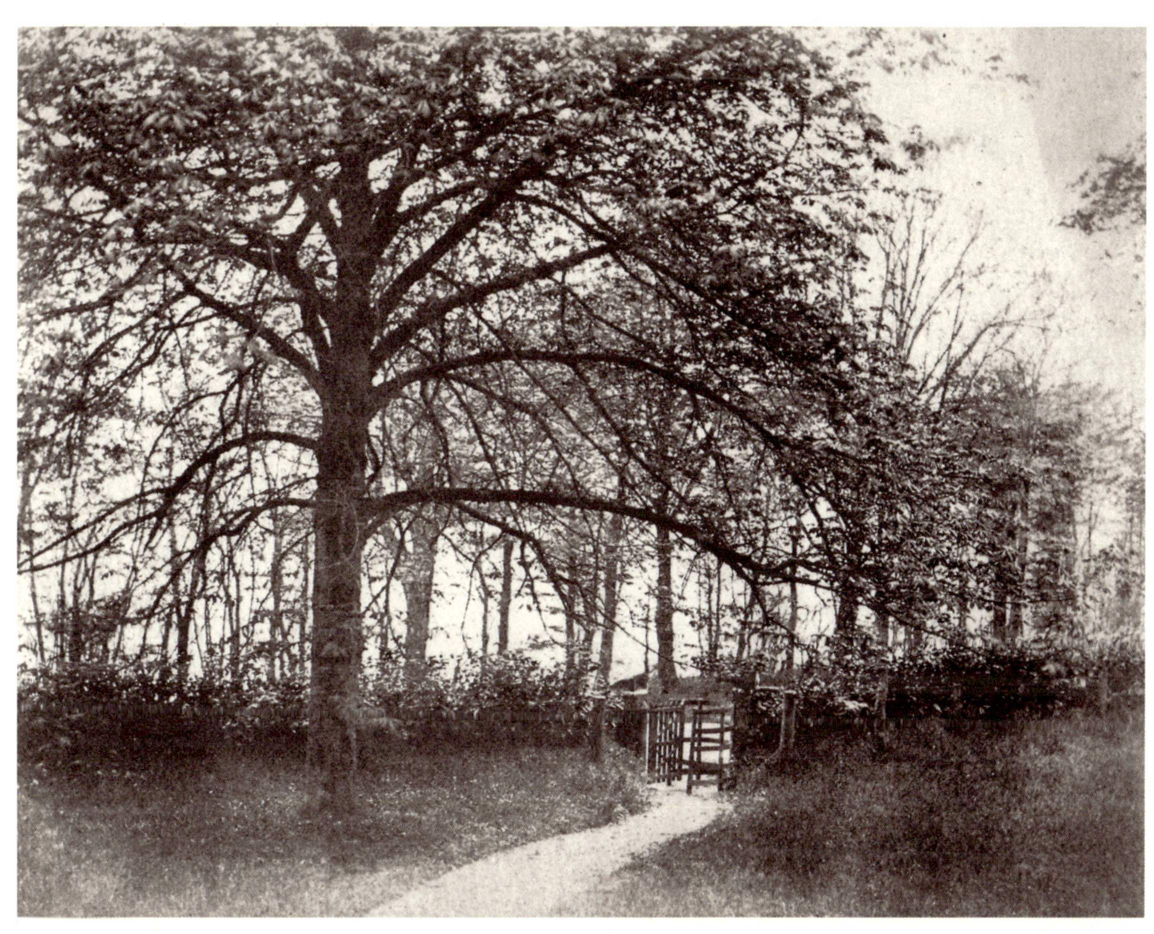

26 **Path and gateway through trees**
salt paper print from a calotype negative
118 × 150 mm
PGP-W100

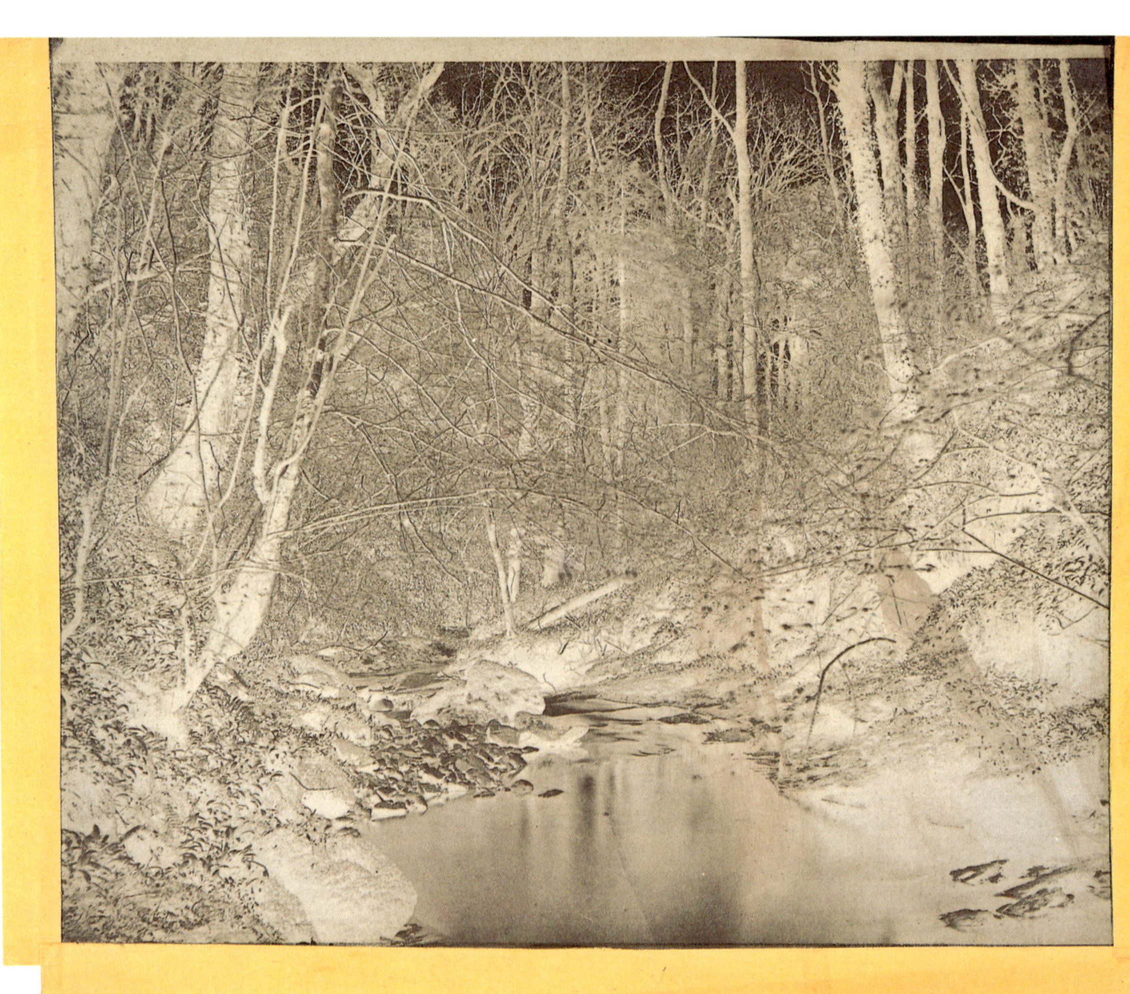

27 **Stream running through wood**
calotype negative with strips of paper round three sides to form 'safe edge' for carbon printing
130 × 157 mm
PGP-W103

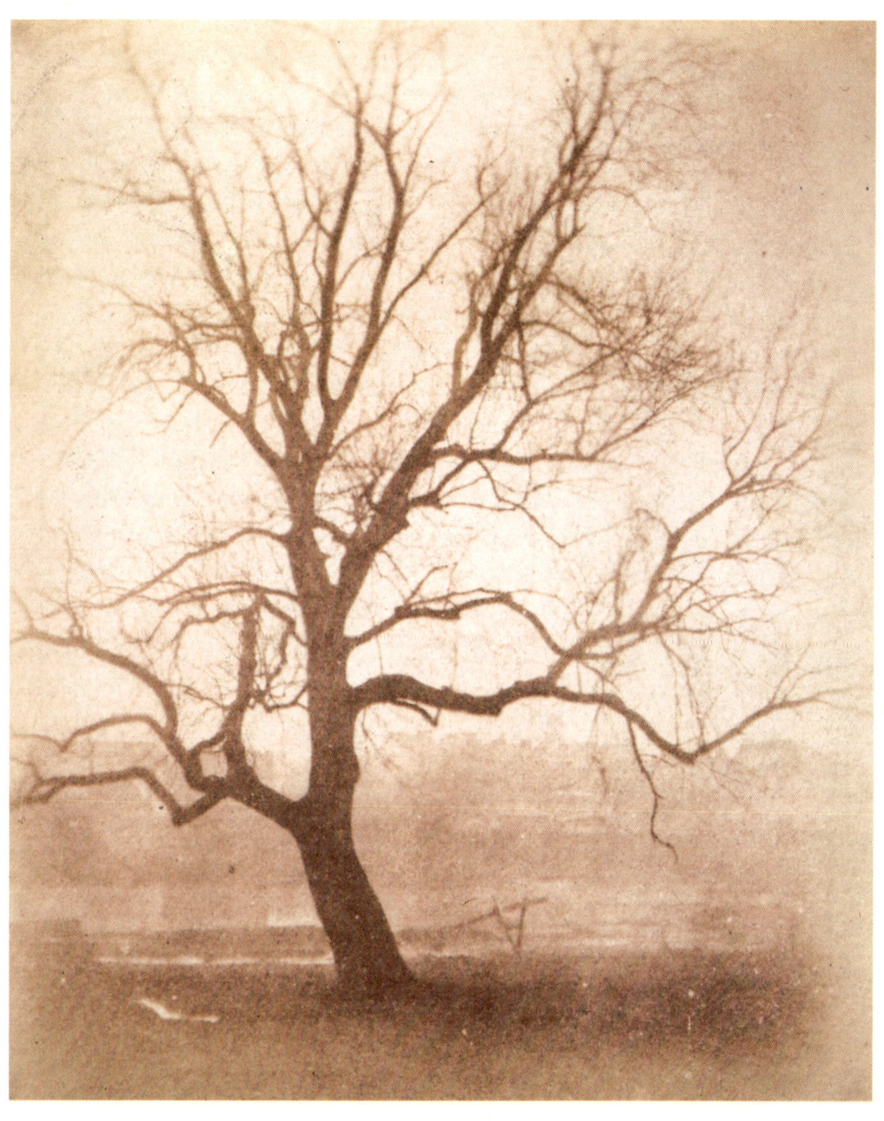

28 **Tree study**
bromide fixed salt paper print from a calotype negative
'Br2 NB'
143 × 115 mm
PGP-W102

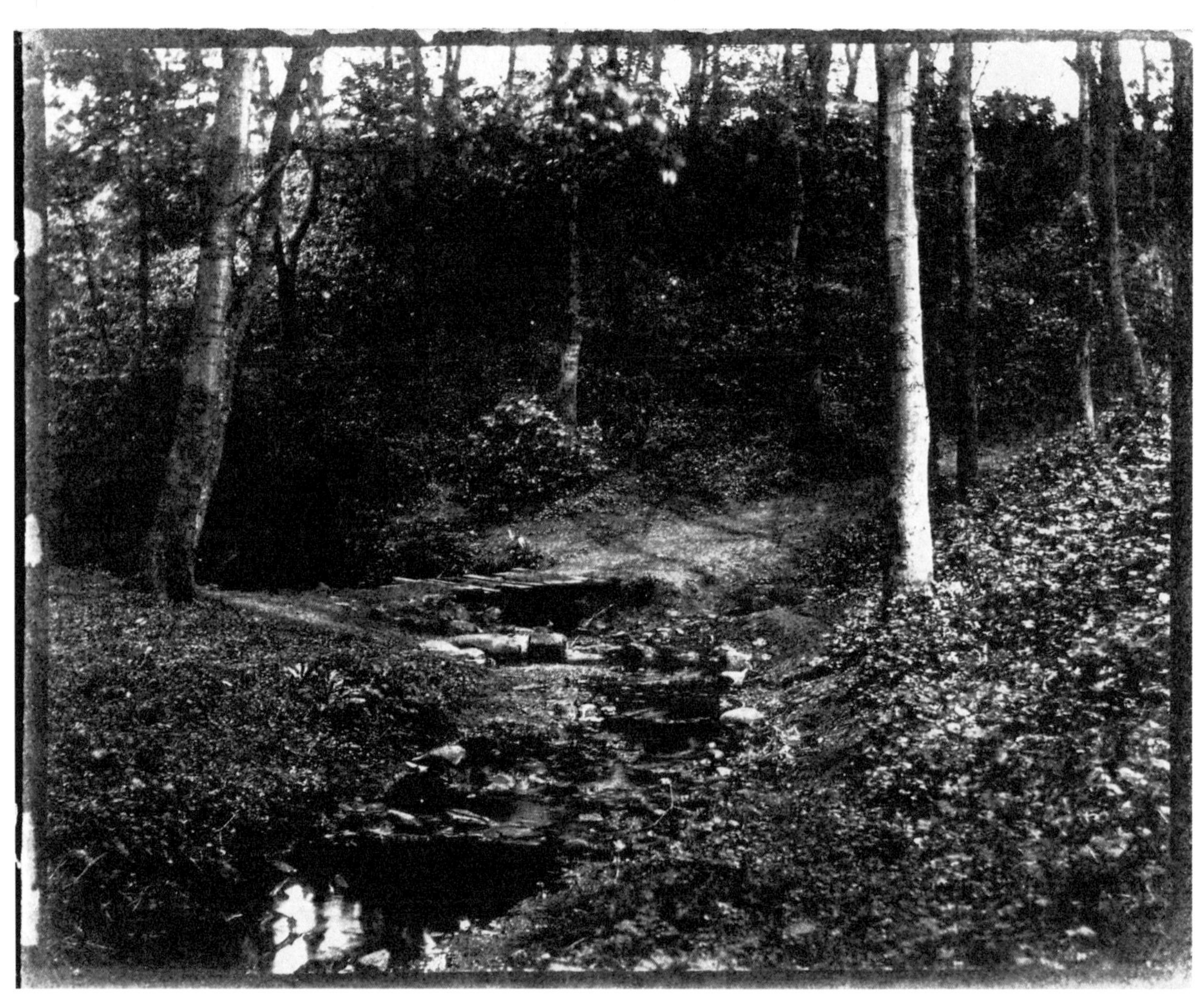

 29 **Fairlie (?)**
salt paper print from a calotype negative
paper, 'J W[HATMAN] TU[RKEY MILL]'
130 × 160 mm
PGP-W104

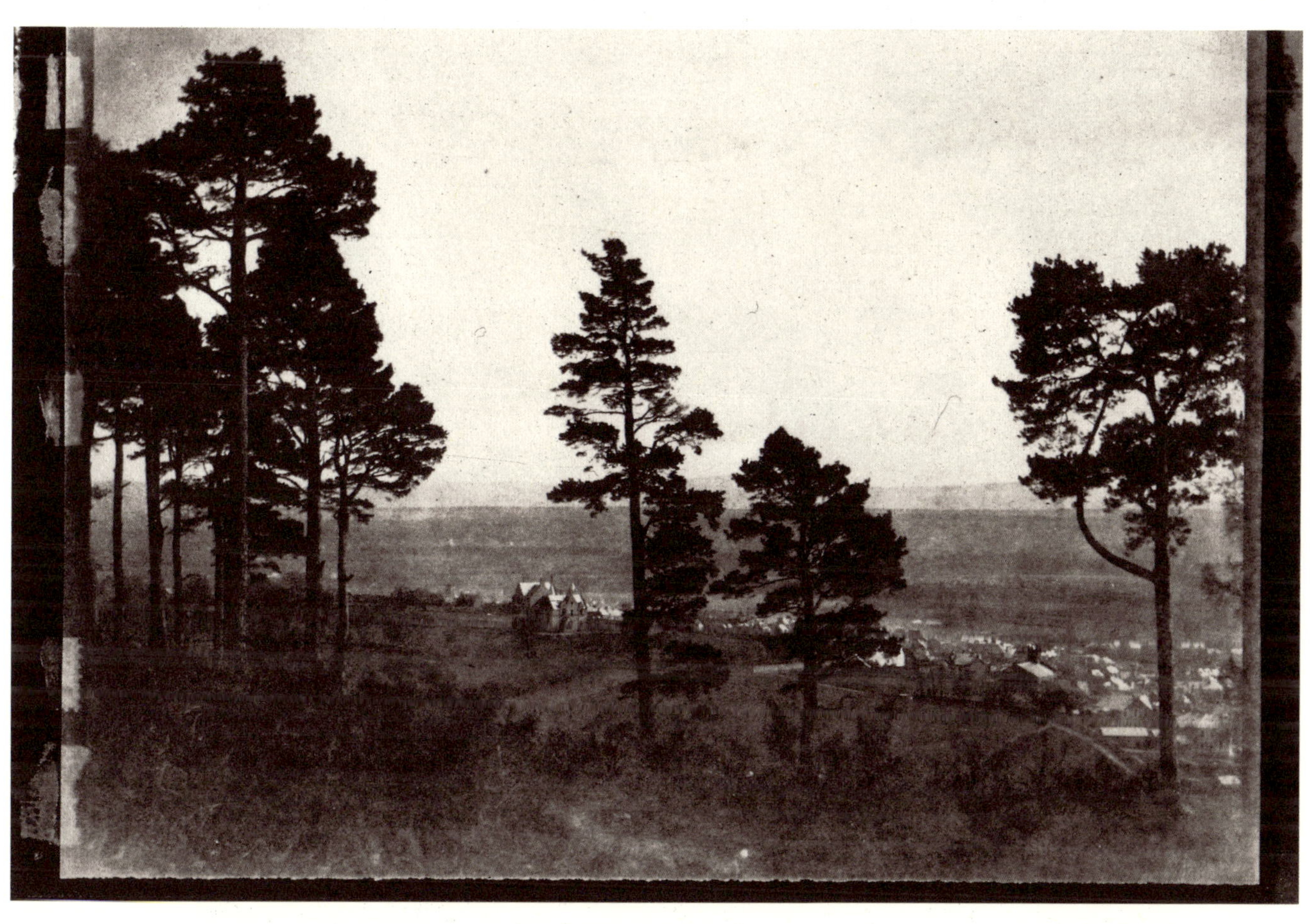

30 **Lamlash, Arran**
salt paper print from a calotype negative
117 × 173 mm
PGP-W98

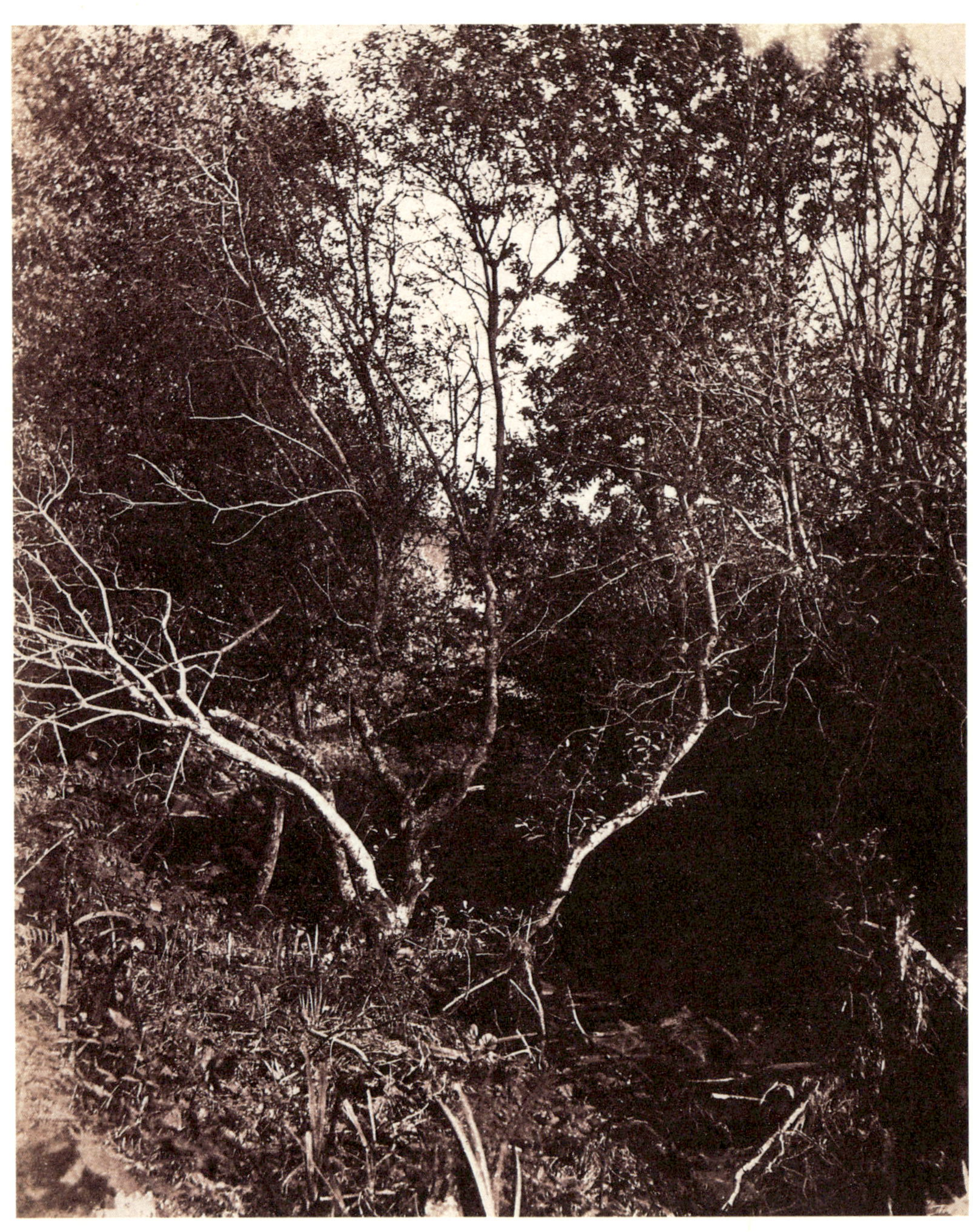

31 **Woodland study**
salt paper print from a calotype negative
167 × 134 mm
PGP-W109

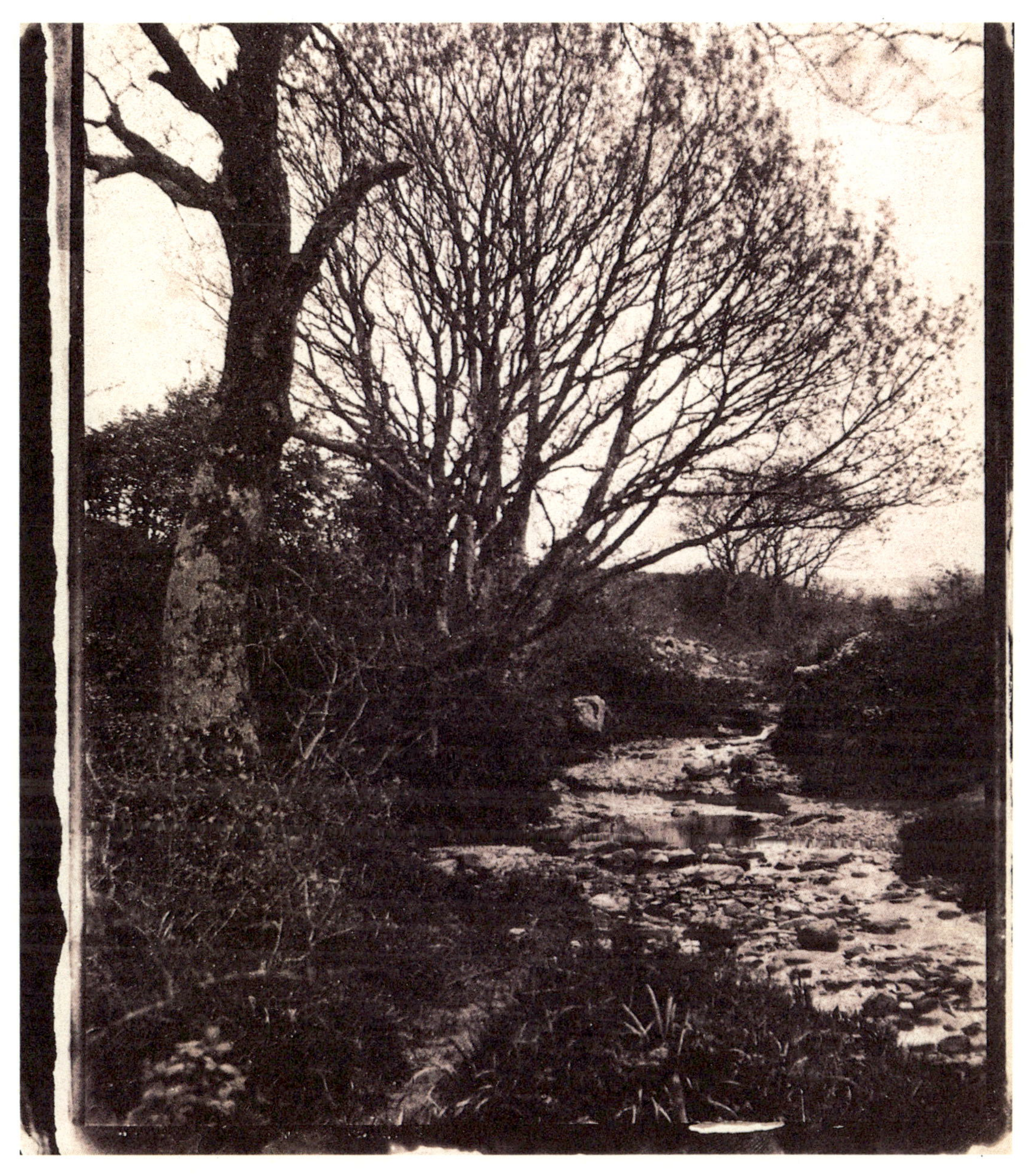

32 **Trees and stream**
salt paper print from a calotype negative
159 x 140 mm
PGP-W110

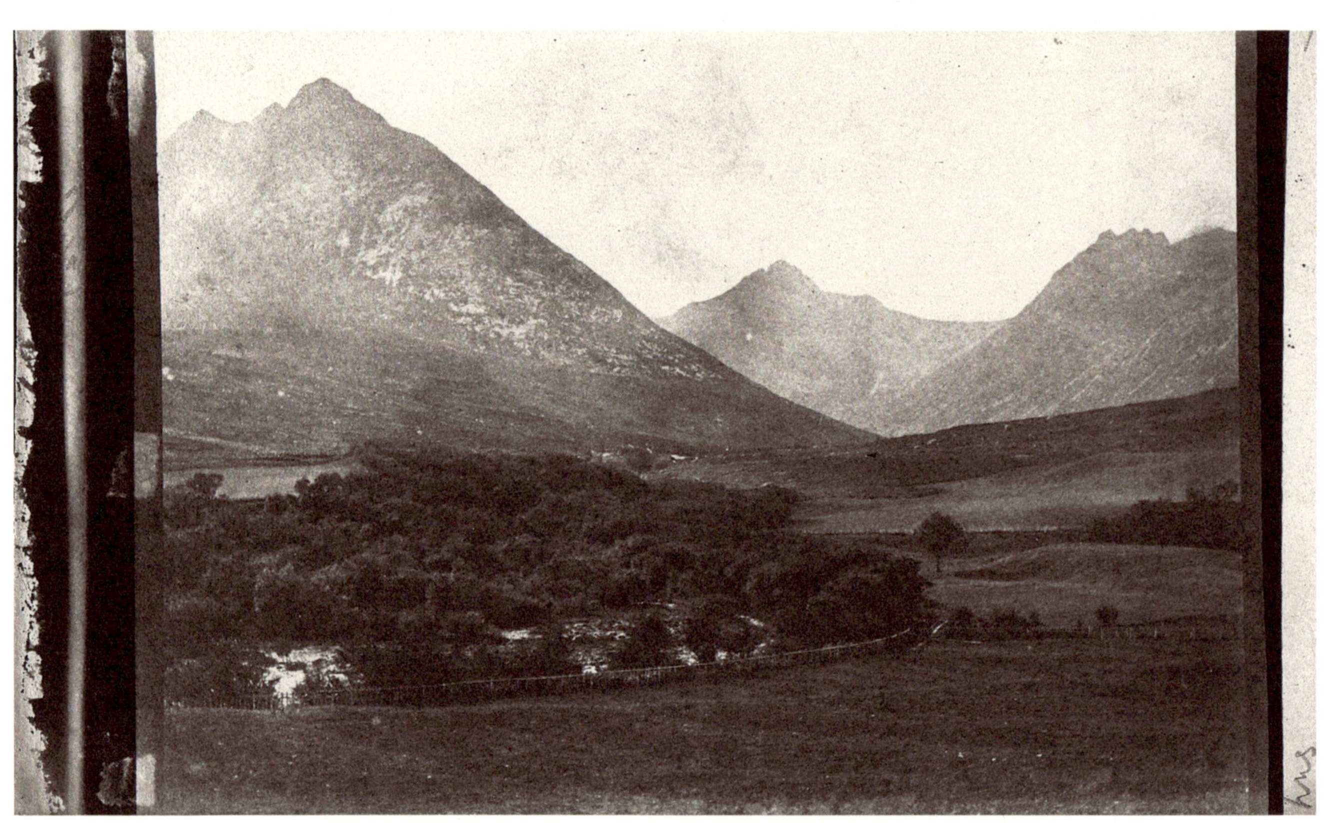

 33 **Sannox, Arran**
salt paper print from a calotype negative
shape of the mountain 'improved' on the negative
'7 / hrs[?]'
114 × 184 mm
PGP-W92

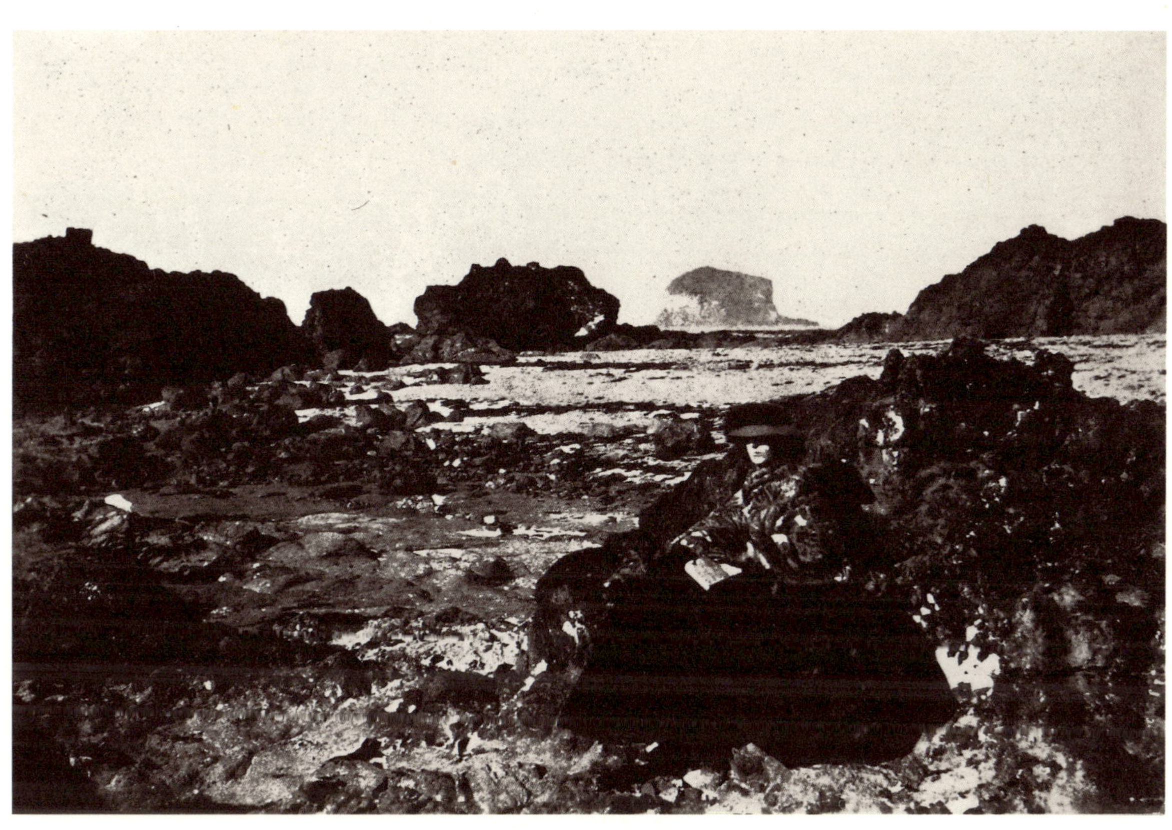

34 **East Lothian shore with the Bass Rock in the distance**
carbon print from a calotype negative
104 × 153 mm
PGP-W60

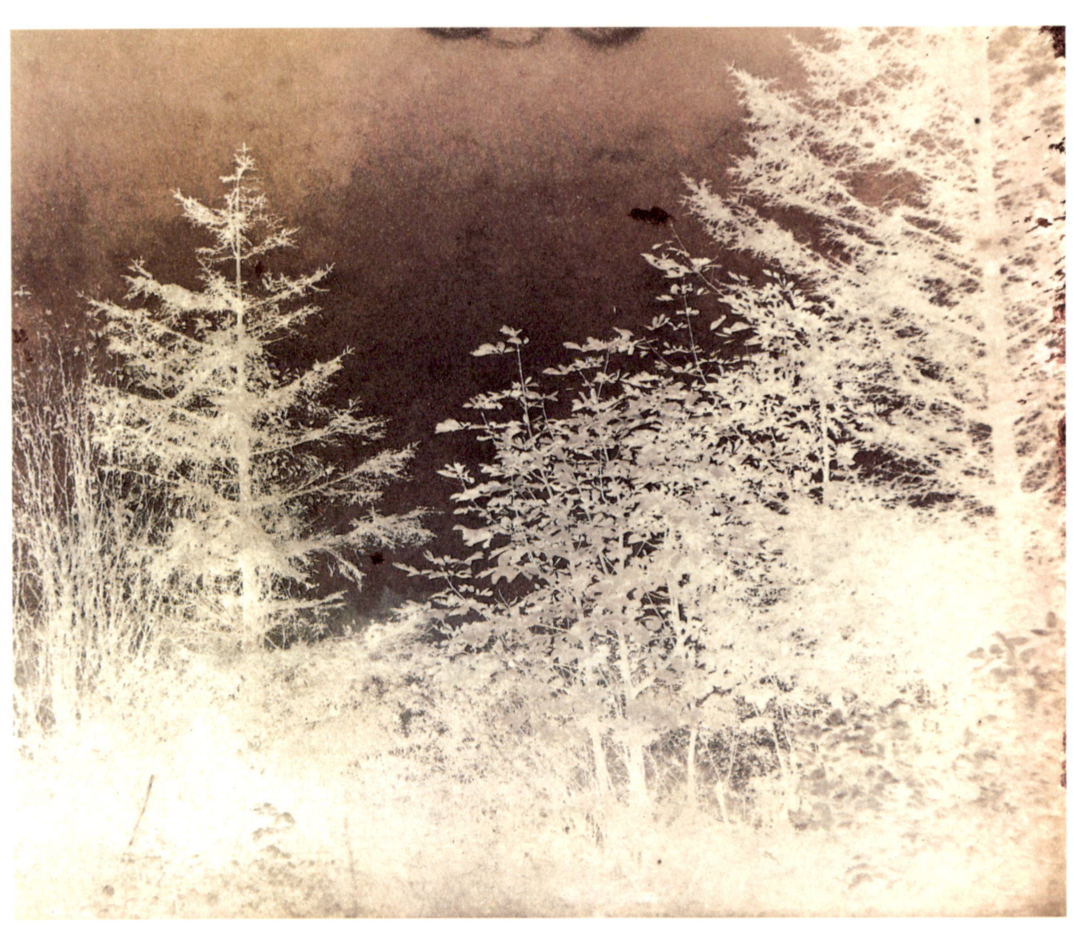

35 **Young trees**
calotype negative, touched up with red ink or watercolour
120 × 140 mm
PGP-W95

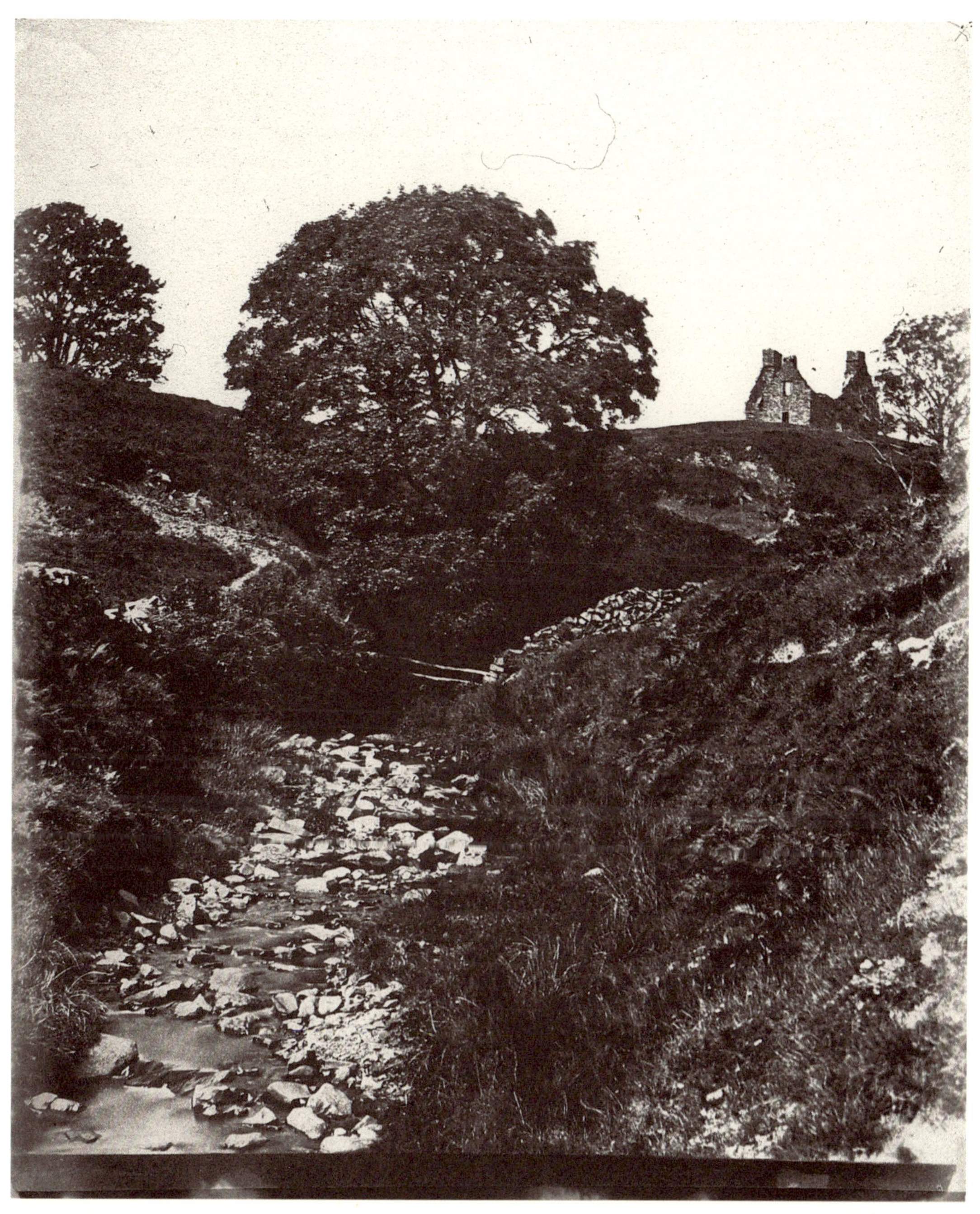

36 **Landscape with ruin**
salt paper print from a calotype negative
'x/W/Cl 15 Am Nit'
240 × 195 mm
PGP-W94

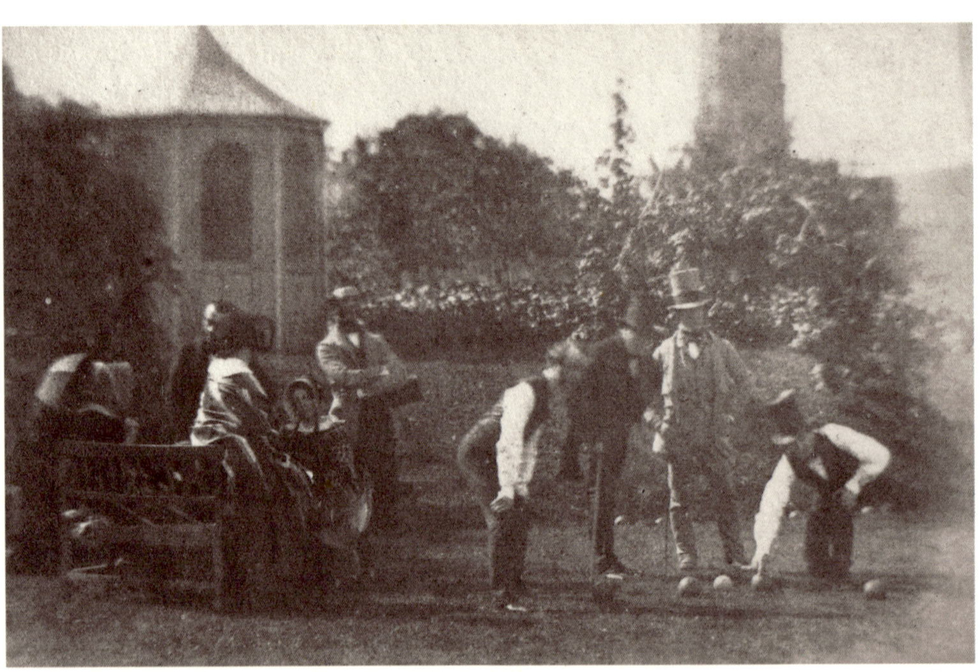

37 **A game of bowls**
toned salt paper print from a calotype negative
'B2/Sta [*or* Stu]'
85 × 129 mm
PGP-W89

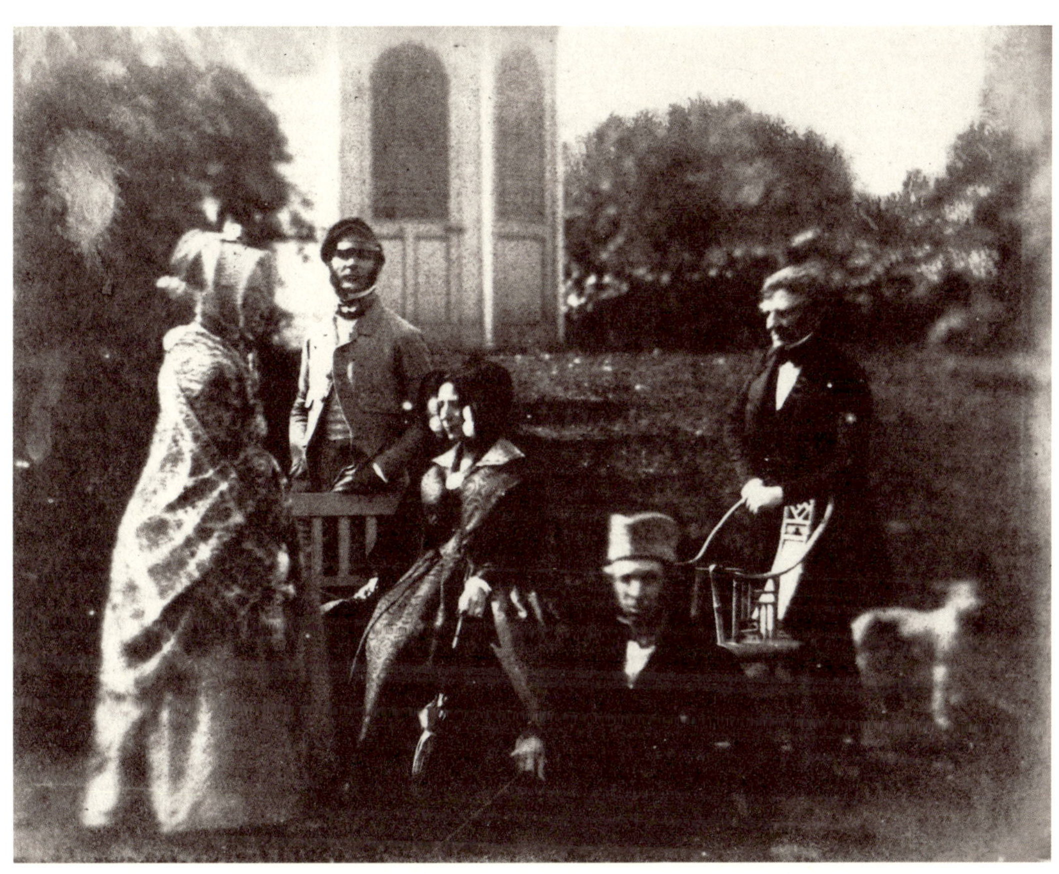

38 **Group at Leith**
toned salt paper print from a calotype negative
'Sta B2'
111 × 138 mm
PGP-W55

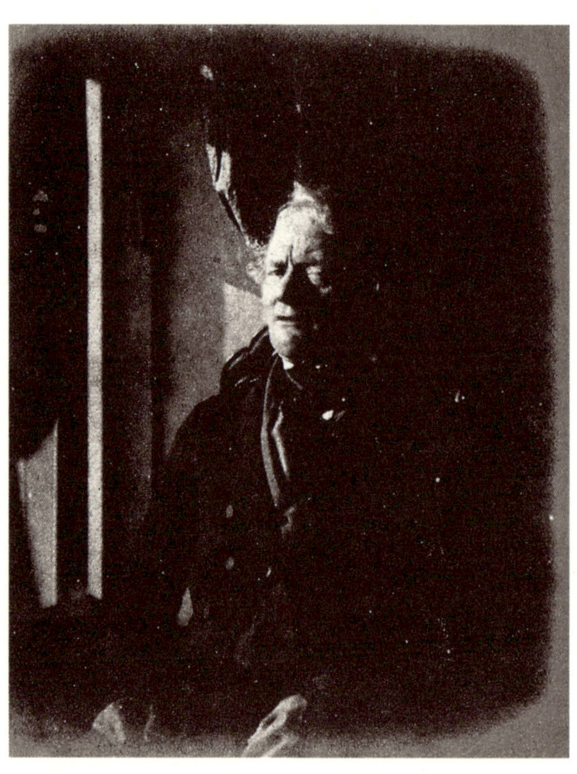

39 **Unknown man, photographed indoors by a window**
salt paper print from a calotype negative
98 × 75 mm
PGP-W47

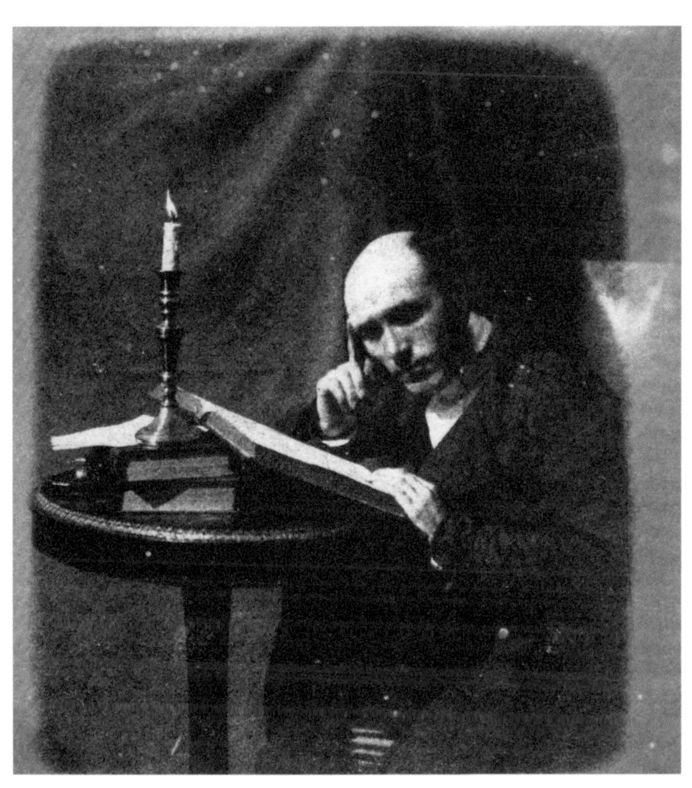

40 **Unknown man reading by candlelight**
copper-toned(?) salt paper print from a calotype negative
candle flame presumably drawn in on the negative
'A Ag — 70 — m [*or* cu] — 1st'
99 × 89 mm
PGP-W41

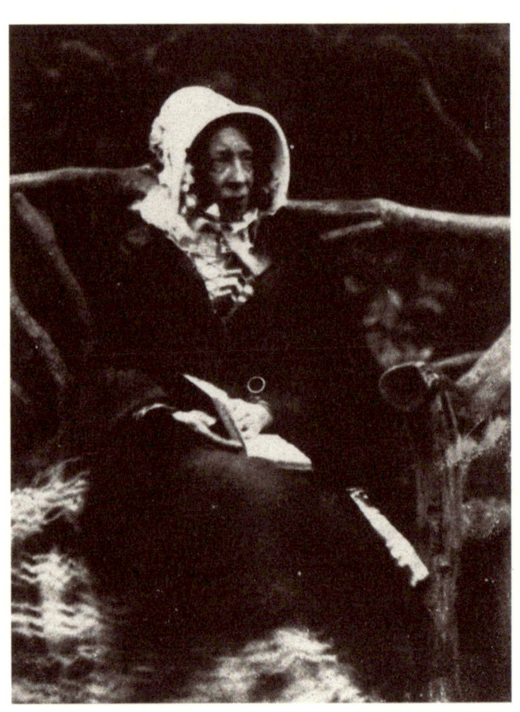

41 **Old woman with book, probably at Leith**
salted paper print from a calotype negative
90 × 67 mm
PGP-W48

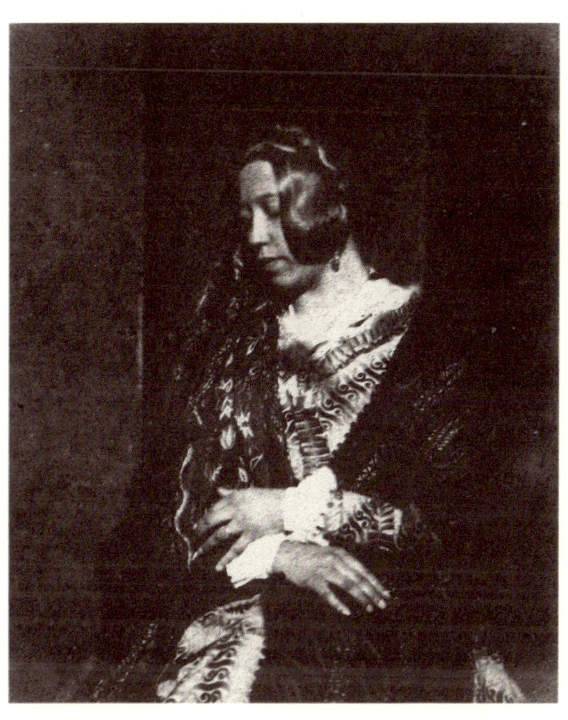

42 **Miss Goldthorpe**
salted paper print from a calotype negative
90 × 73 mm
PGP-W49

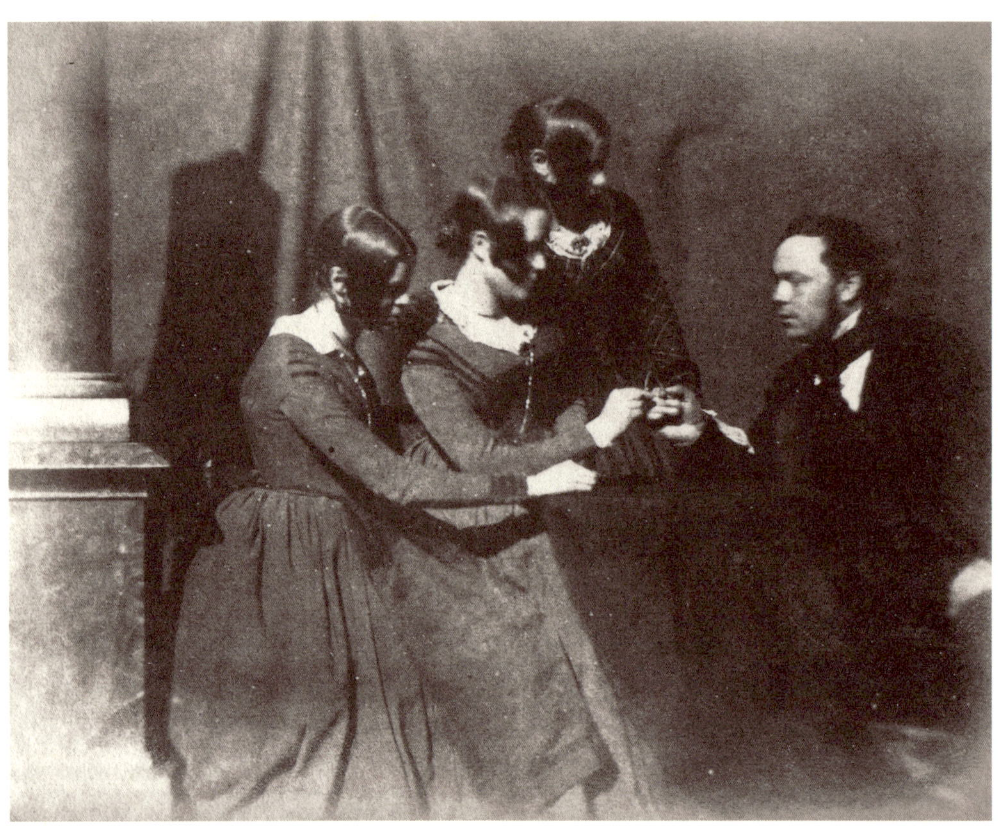

43 **Mr Purdie and his friends pulling a wishbone**
copper-toned salt paper print from a calotype negative
'S ['c' in reverse] Ag 70 co last'
106 x 131 mm
PGP-W54

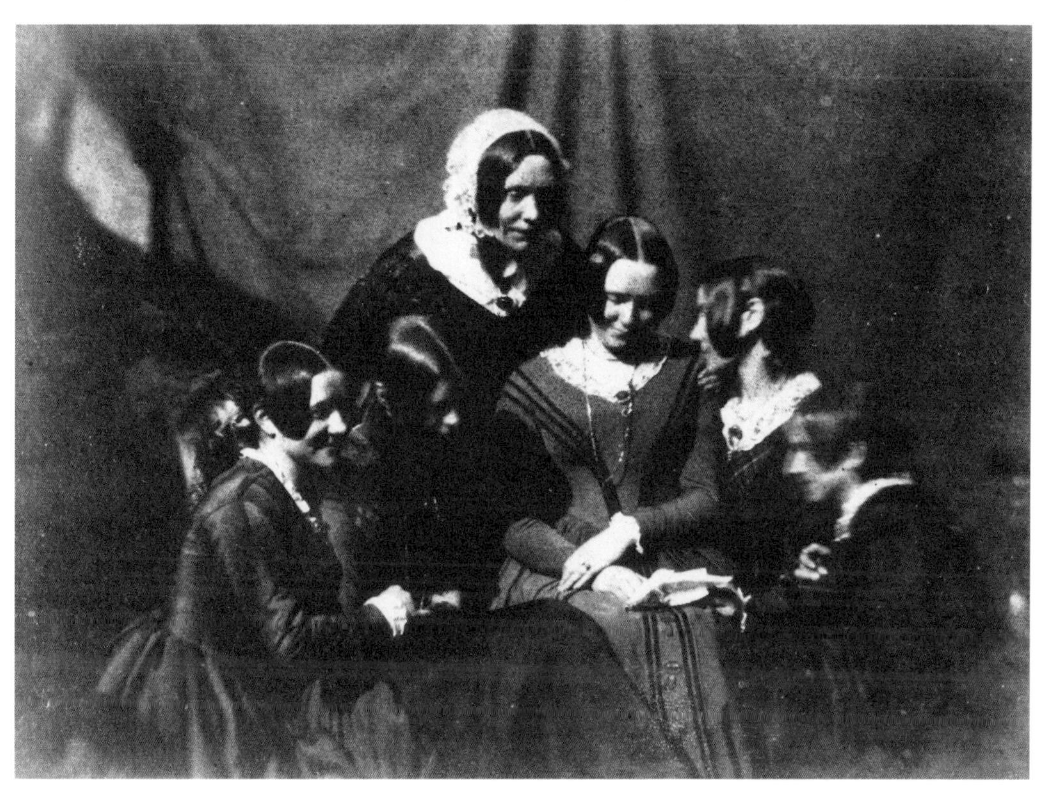

44 **Group of women with a letter**
salt paper print from a calotype negative
'W / JMW'
100 × 135 mm
PGP-W78

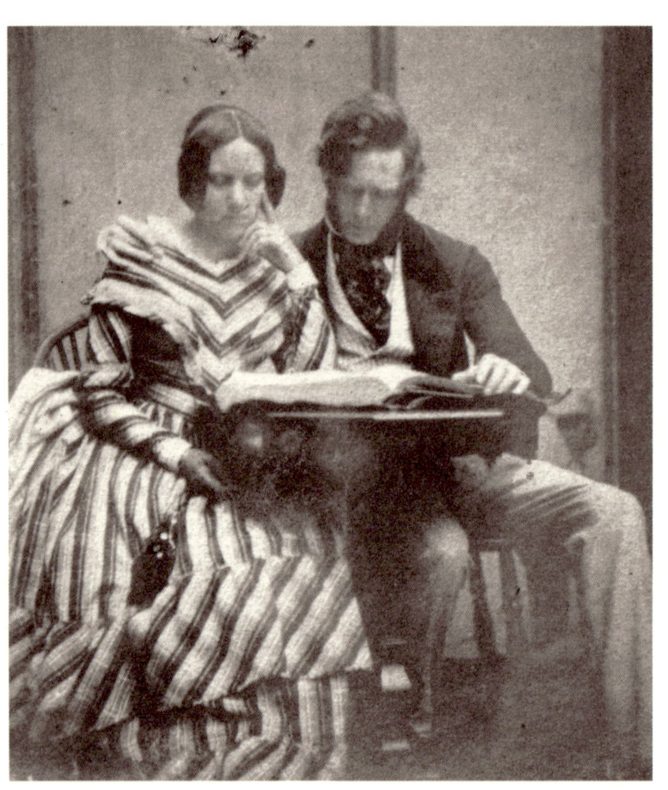

45 **Lucy and Henry Cundell**
salt paper print from a calotype negative
'A Cl[?] Ag — 70'
100 × 86 mm
PGP-W50

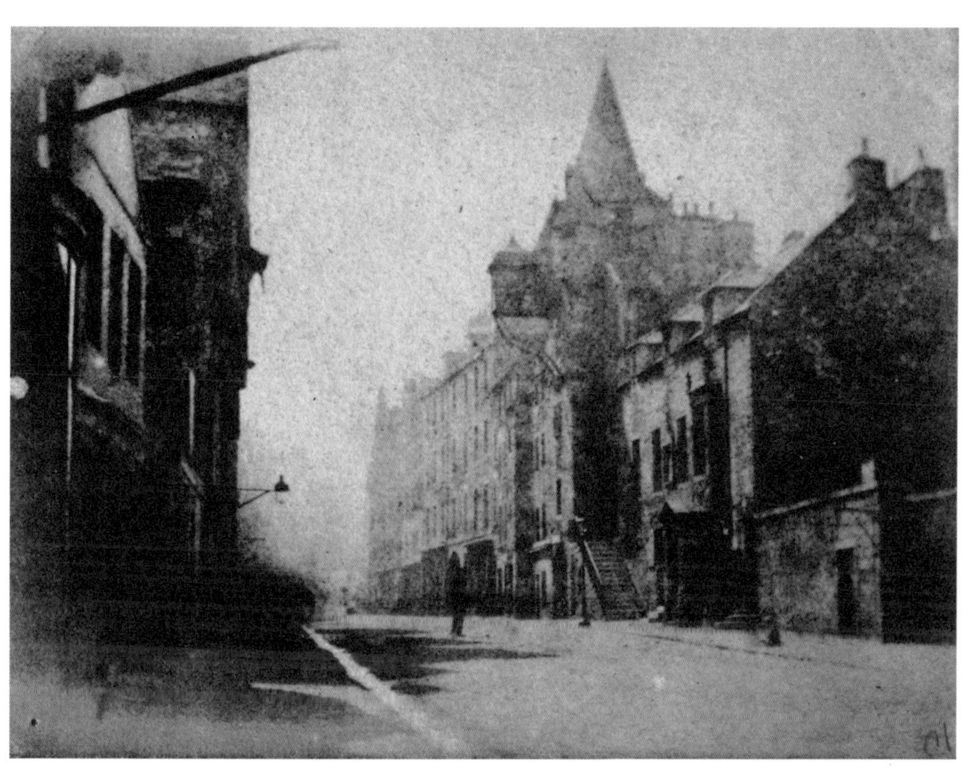

46 **The Canongate Tolbooth, Edinburgh High Street**
salt paper print from a calotype negative
'01'
97 × 126 mm
PGP-W84

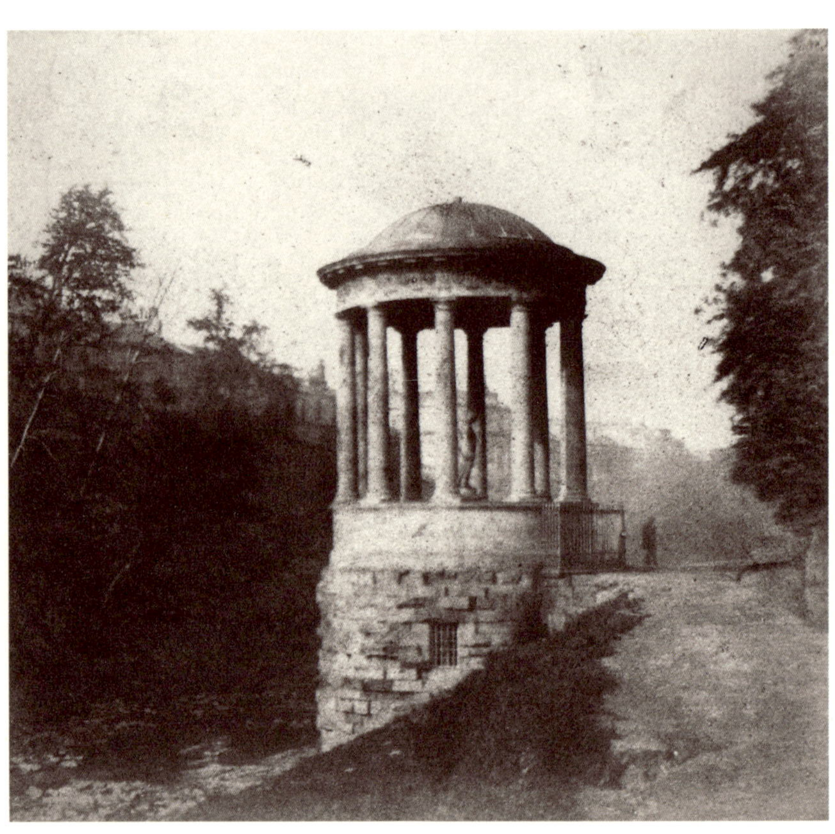

47 **St Bernard's Well, Water of Leith, Edinburgh**
gold-toned salt paper print from a calotype negative
'? Old Copy — Gold', written in later hand
paper, '[COUN]SELL'
105 × 110 mm
PGP-W87

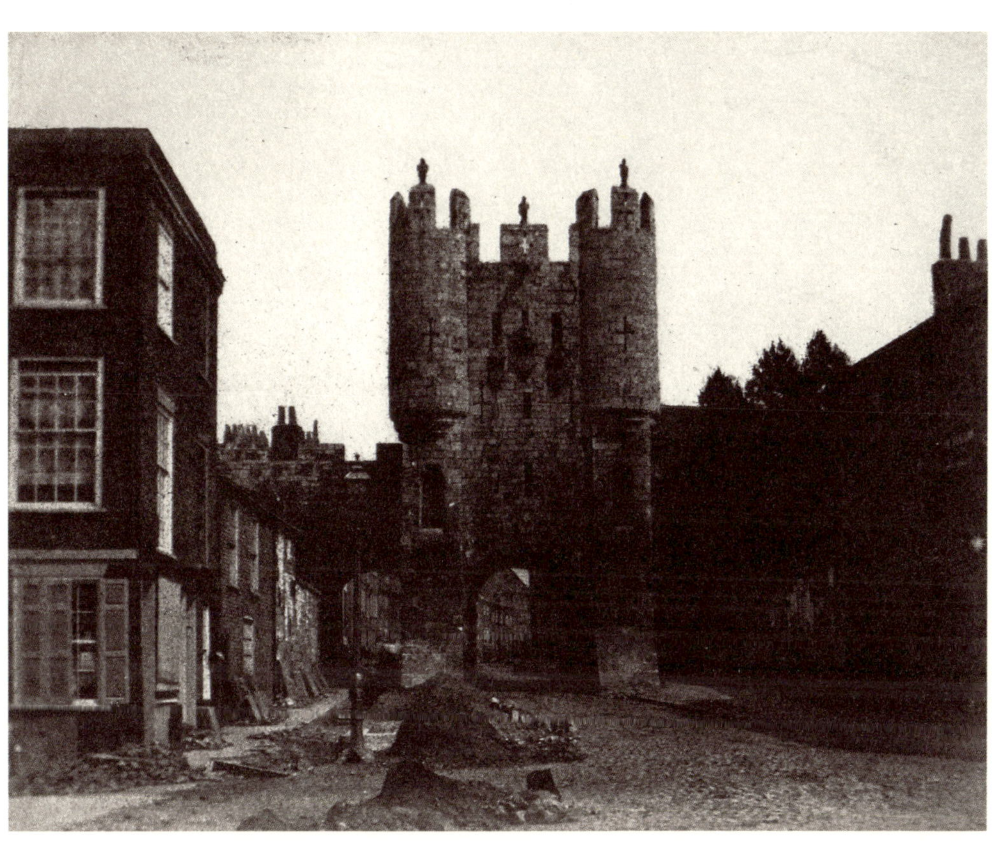

48 **Bootham Bar, York, 19 July 1847**
gold-toned salt paper print from a calotype negative
'Old copy — Gold 64'
106 × 130 mm
PGP-W83

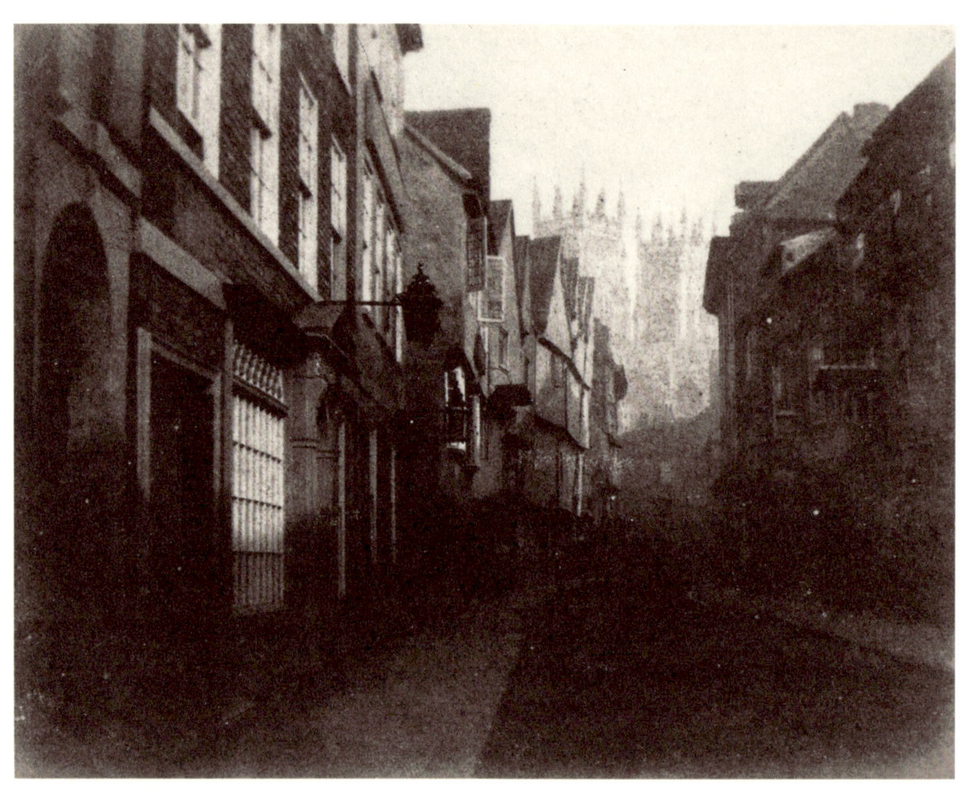

49 **York, view towards the Minster, 19 July 1847**
salt paper print from a calotype negative
100 × 125 mm
PGP-W90

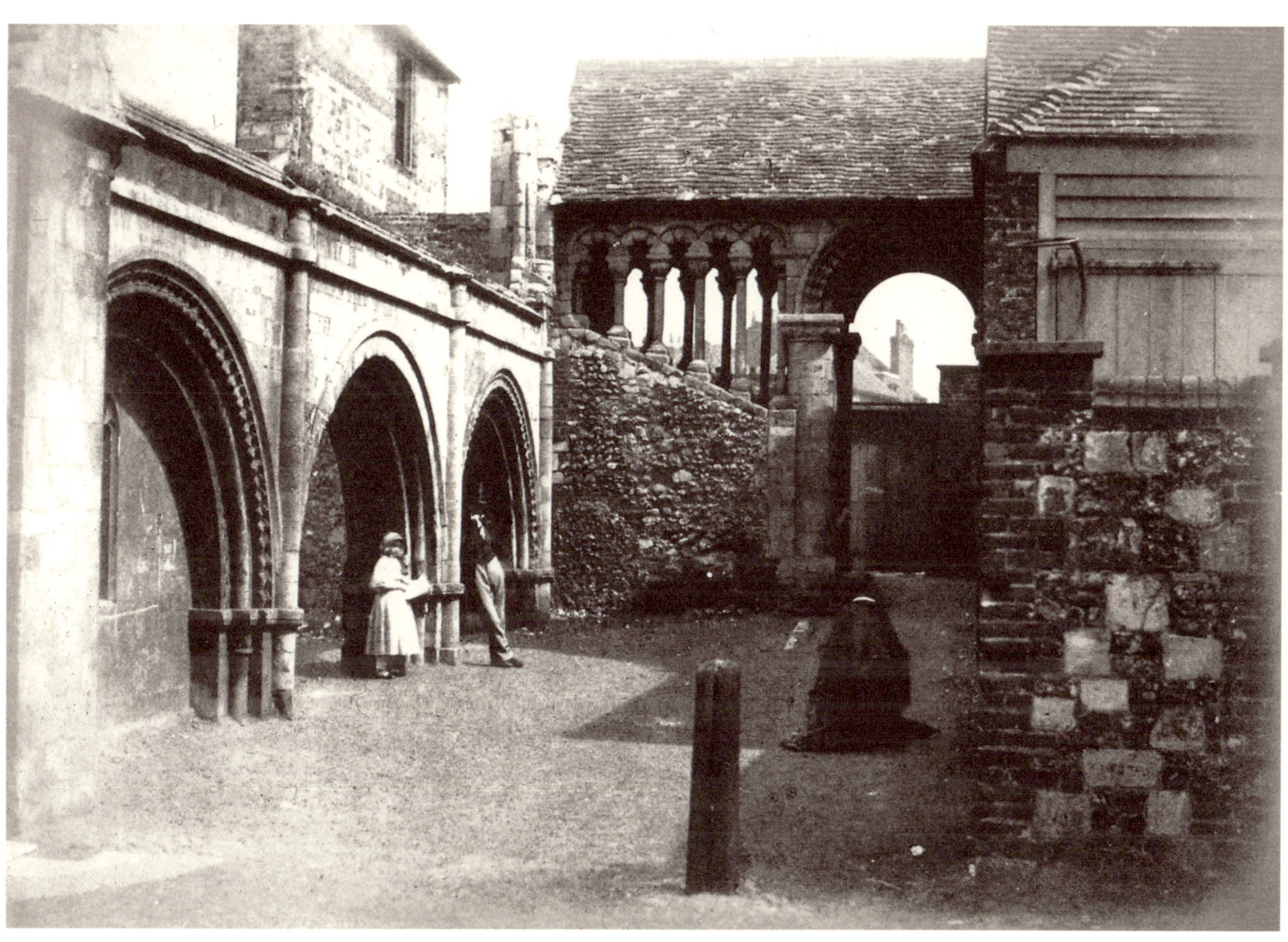

50 **Canterbury**
salt paper print from a calotype negative
165 × 230 mm
PGP-W65

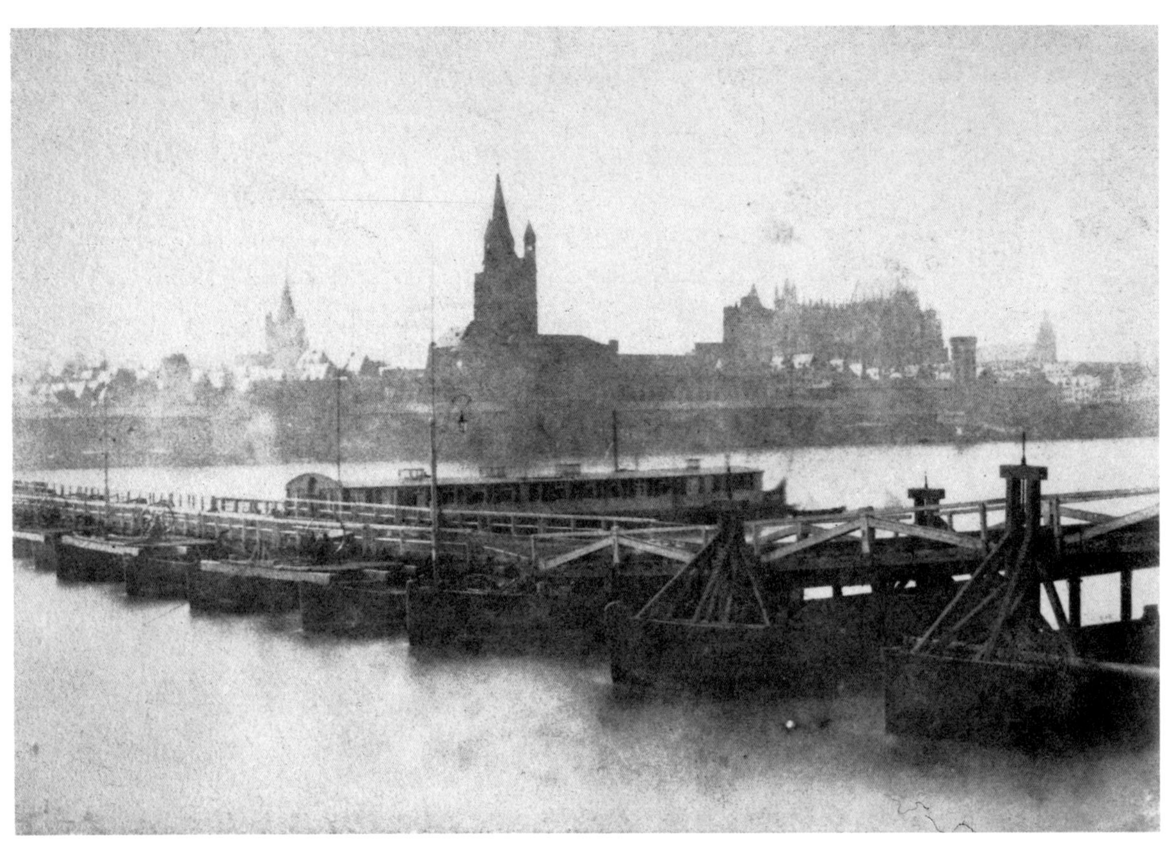

51 **The Rhine at Cologne, probably 1847**
salt paper print from a calotype negative
'3'
107 × 166 mm
PGP-W57

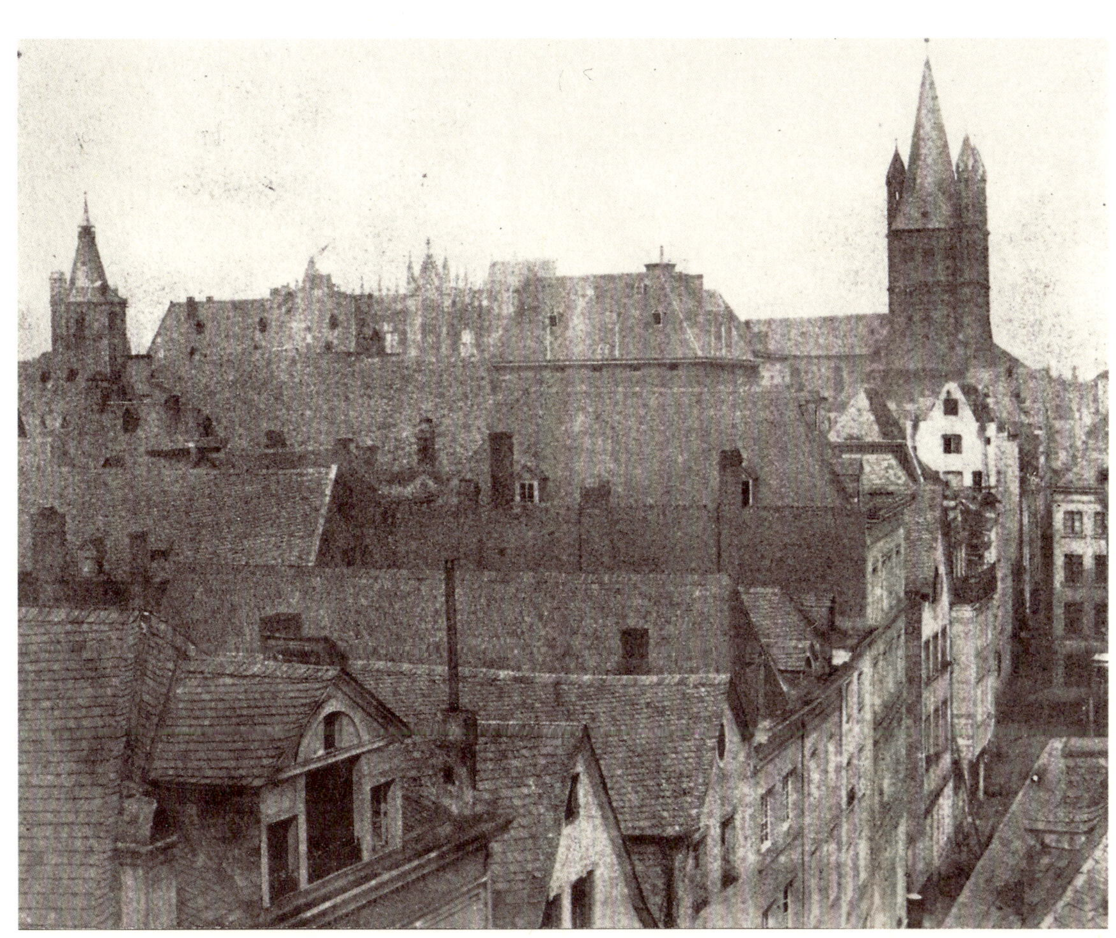

52 **View over the rooftops, Cologne, probably 1847**
salt paper print from a calotype negative
118 × 145 mm
PGP-W73

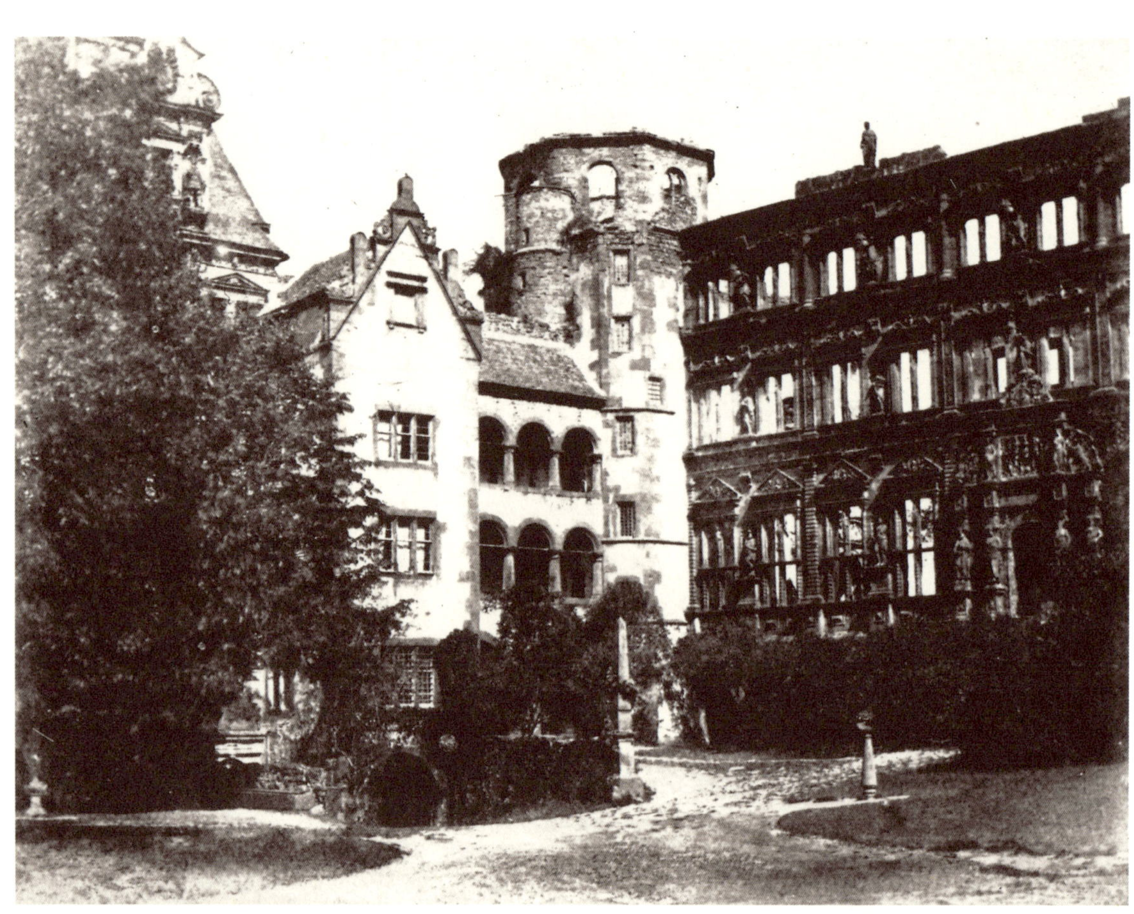

53 **Heidelberg, probably 1847**
salt paper print from a calotype negative
paper, 'J WH[ATMAN] TURKE[Y MILL]'
115 × 148 mm
PGP-W72

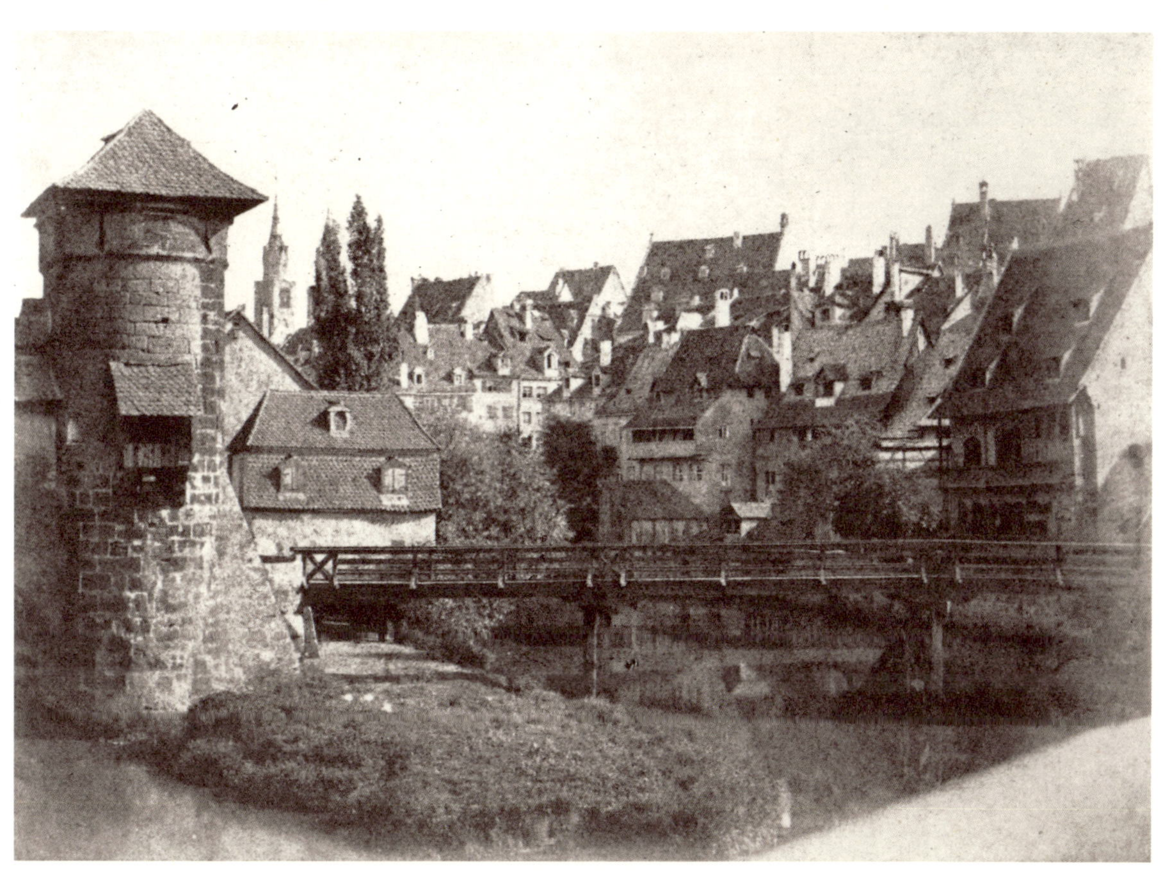

54 **Nuremberg, probably 1847**
salt paper print from a calotype negative
110 × 151 mm
PGP-W71

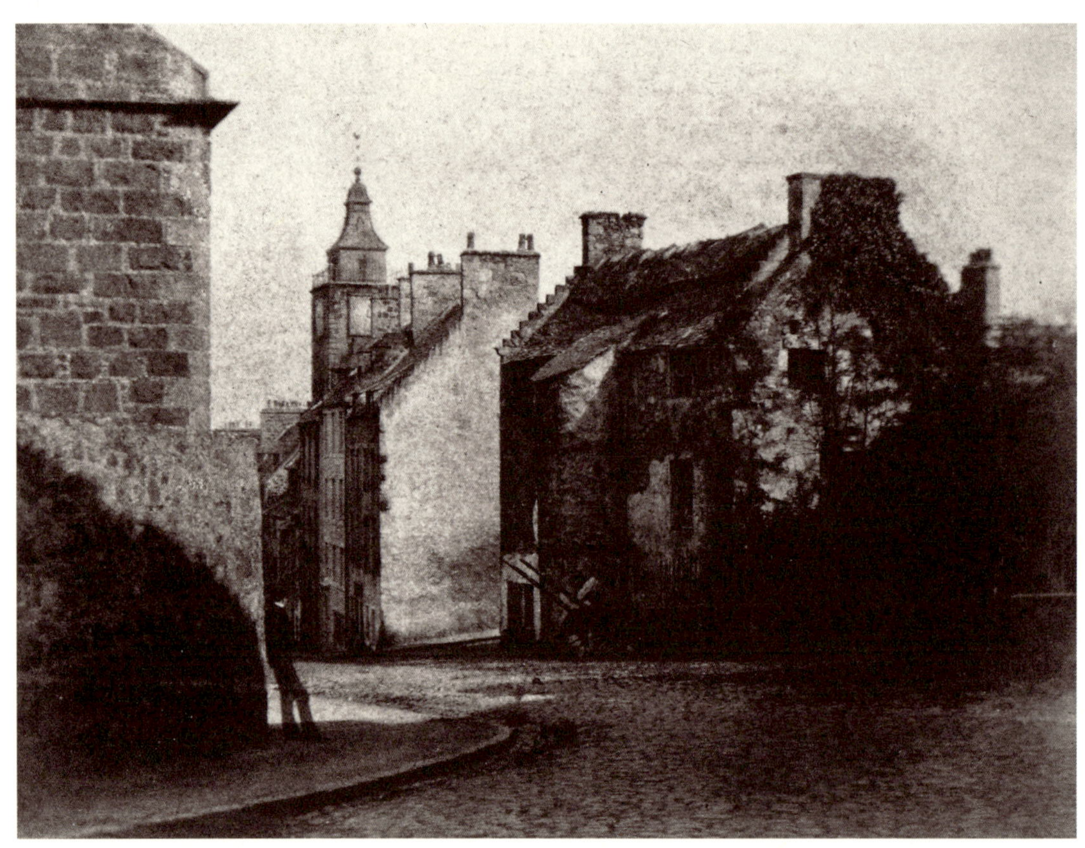

55 **Stirling**
gold-toned salt paper print from a calotype negative
'W / Gold after fixation'
paper, '[WHA]TMAN [TURKE]Y MILL [18]41'
108 × 141 mm
PGP-W85

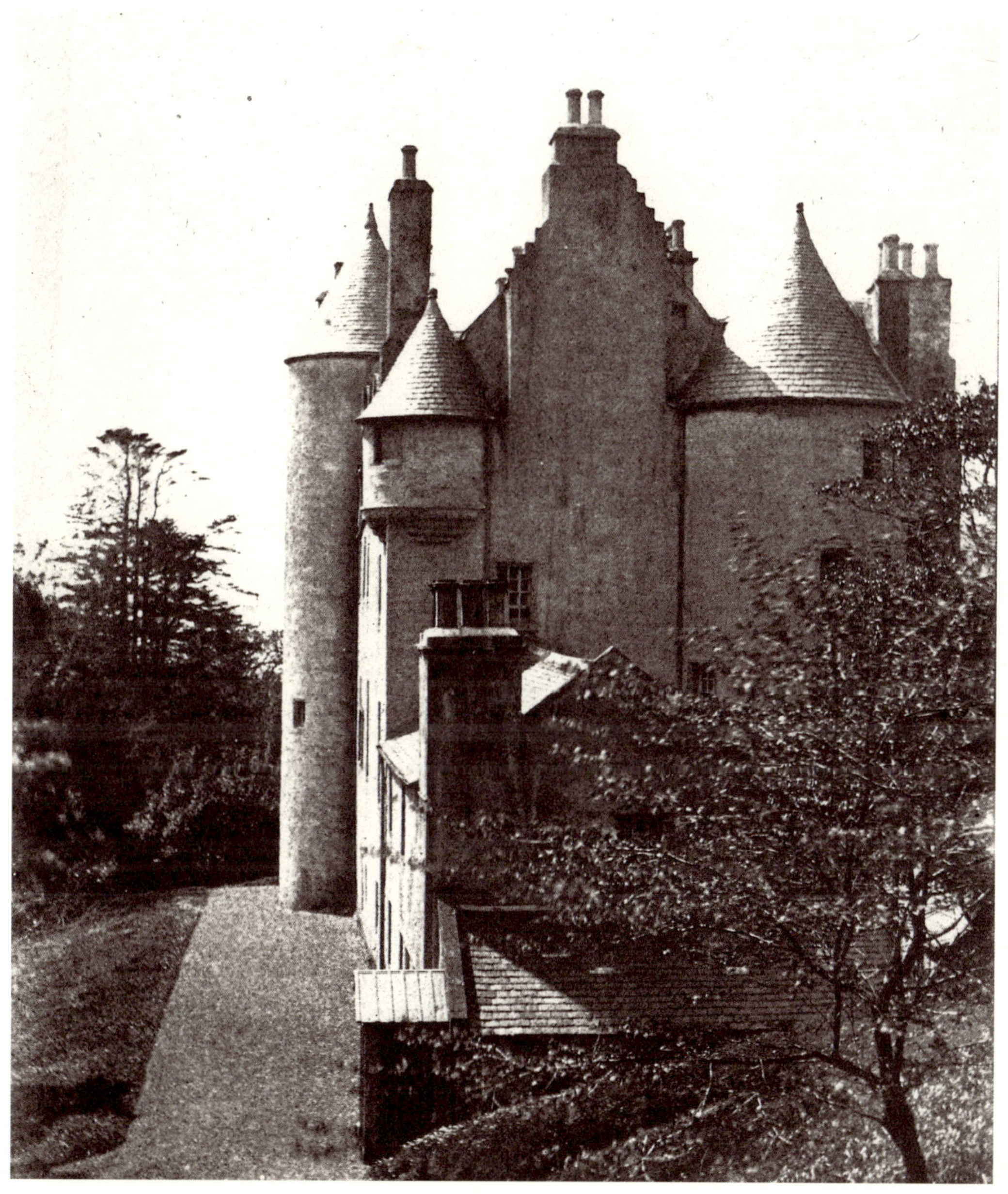

56 **Kelburn Castle**
salt paper print from a calotype negative
paper, 'J WHA[TMAN] TURKEY[MILL]',
'MARION' watermark printed off from negative
160 × 135 mm
PGP-W59

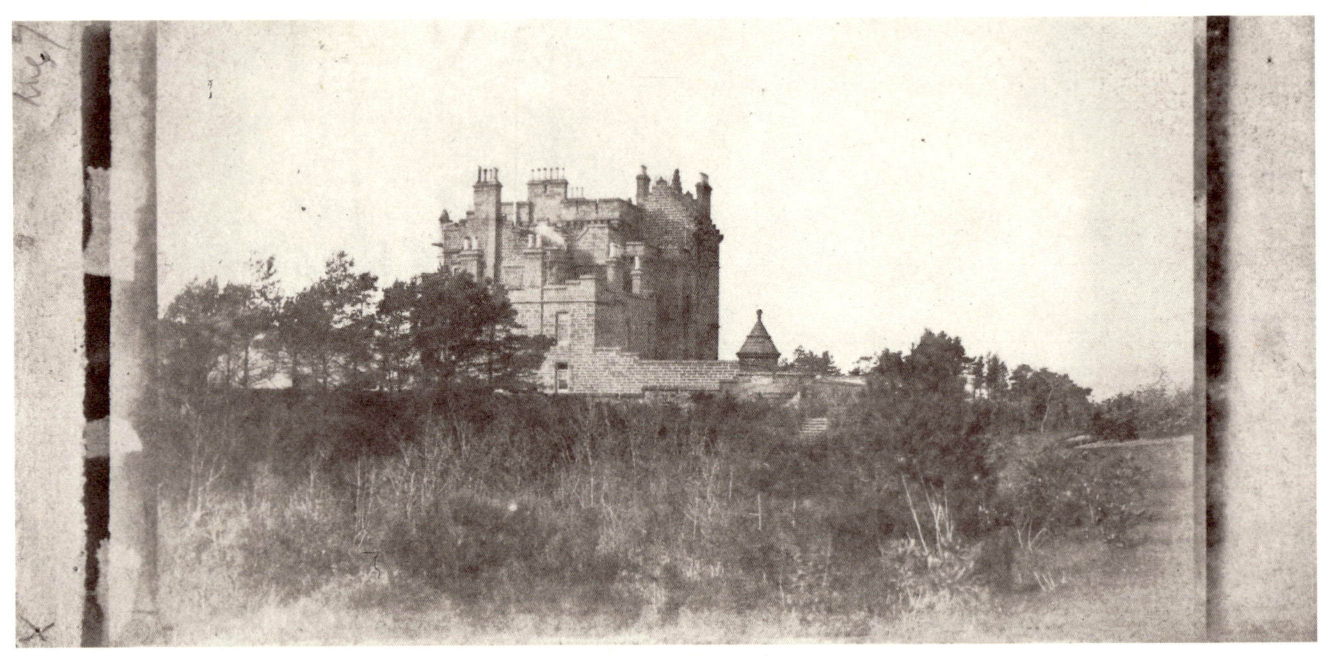

 57 **Culzean Castle**
salt paper print from a calotype negative
'line [*or* hue] 7 / x'
95 × 194 mm
PGP-W61

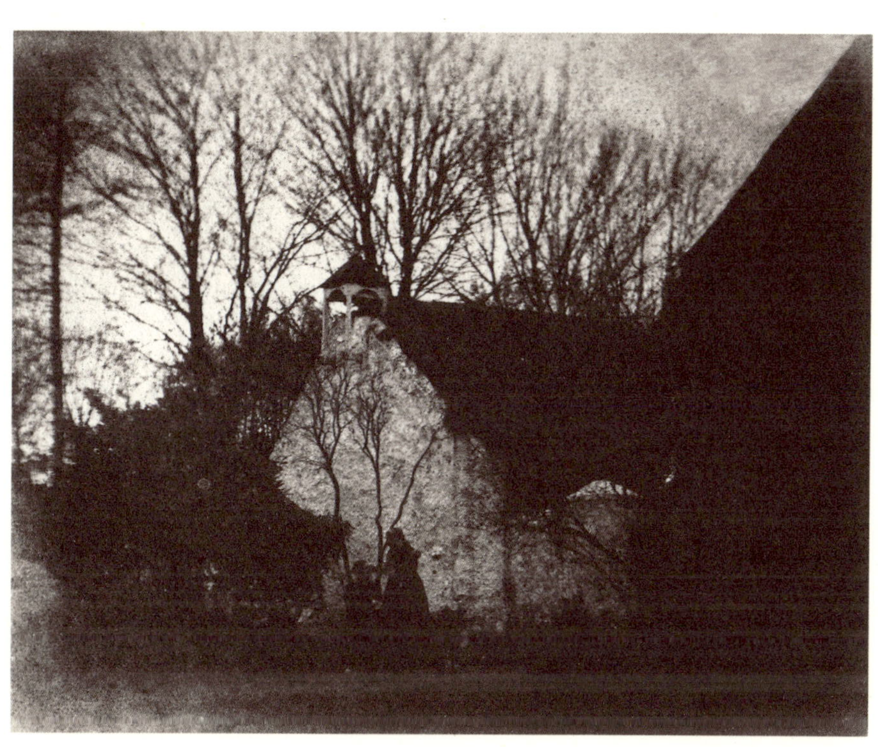

58 **A stable block with the Misses Bennet**
salt paper print from a calotype negative
'W/ A Ag 40'
93 x 104 mm
PGP-W88

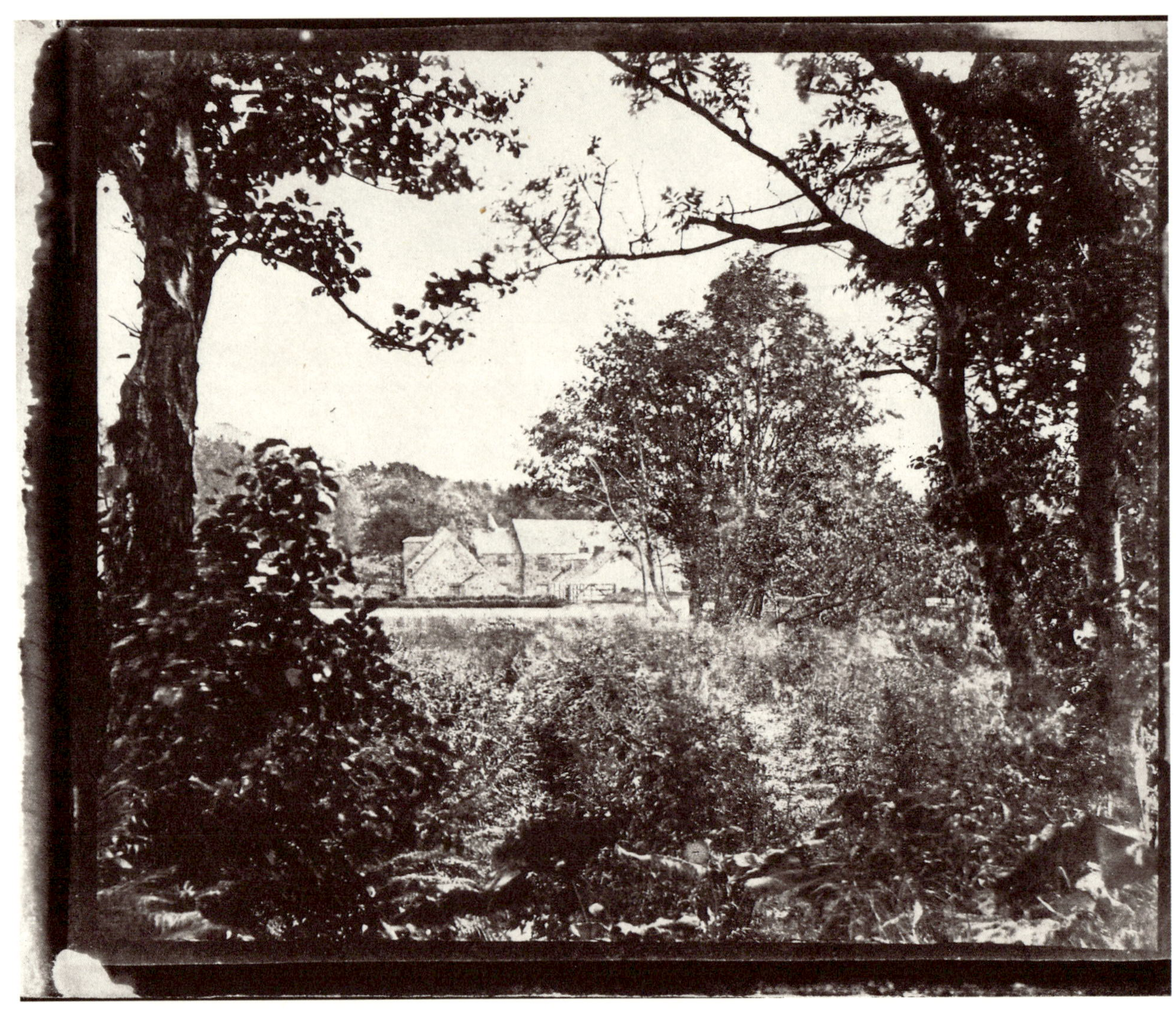

[88] 59 **Brisbane Mains**
salt paper print from a calotype negative
'x'
140 × 165 mm
PGP-W99

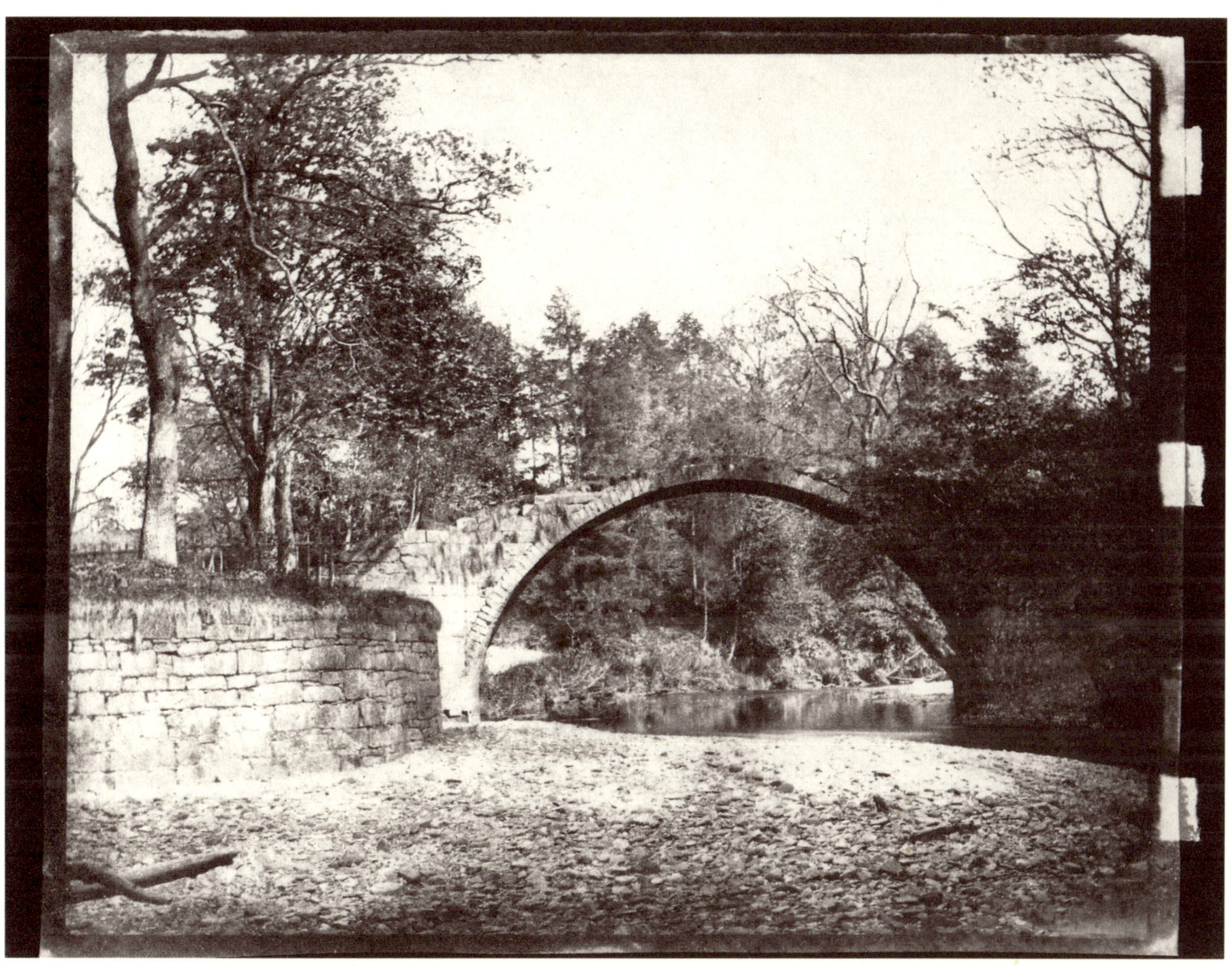

60 **A bridge**
salt paper print from a calotype negative
133 × 177 mm
PGP-W58

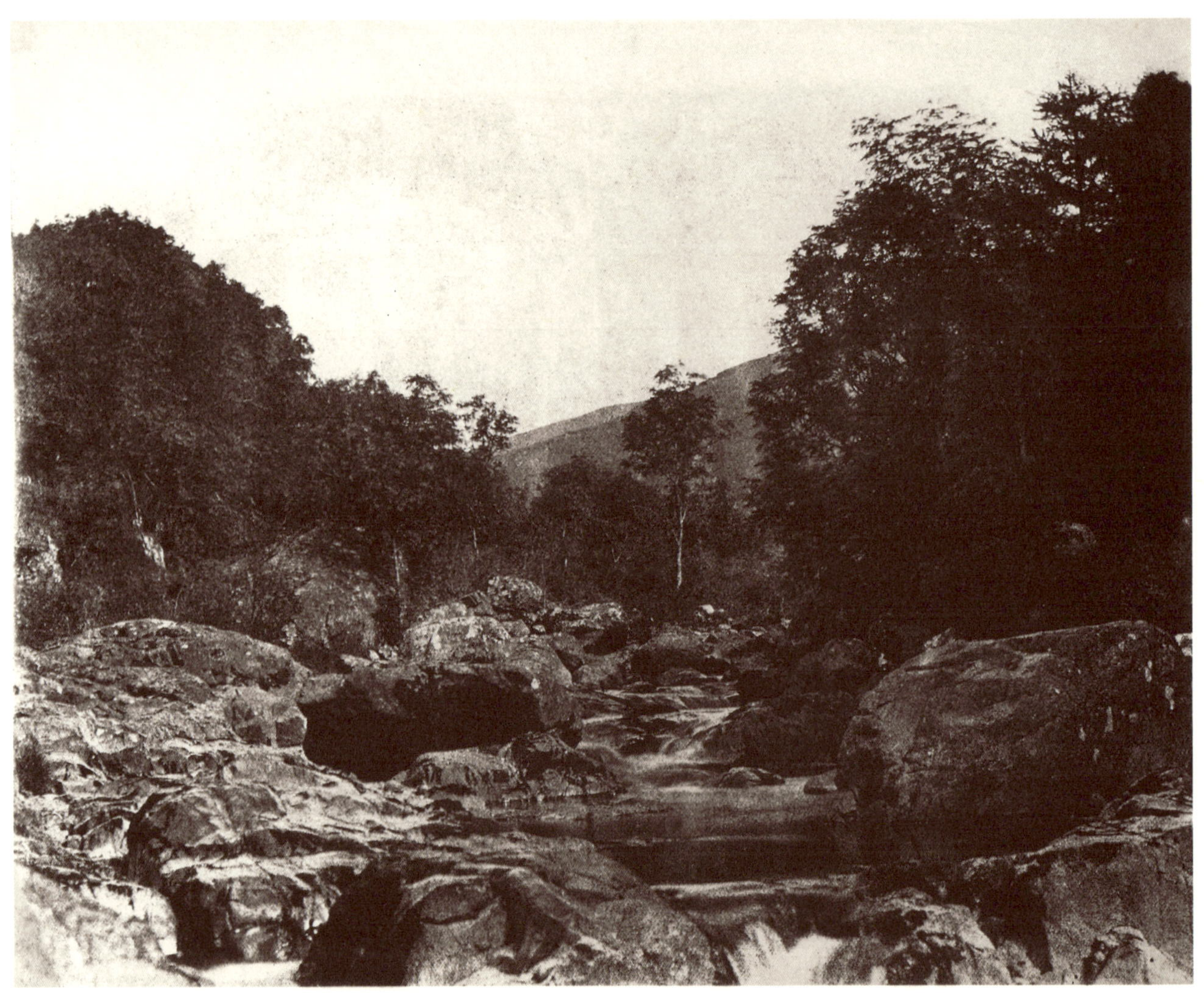

 61 **River bed**
salt paper print from a calotype negative
'Cl 6SMR[?] Am Nit'
paper, 'J WHATMAN TURKEY MILL 1841'
195 x 240 mm
PGP-W105

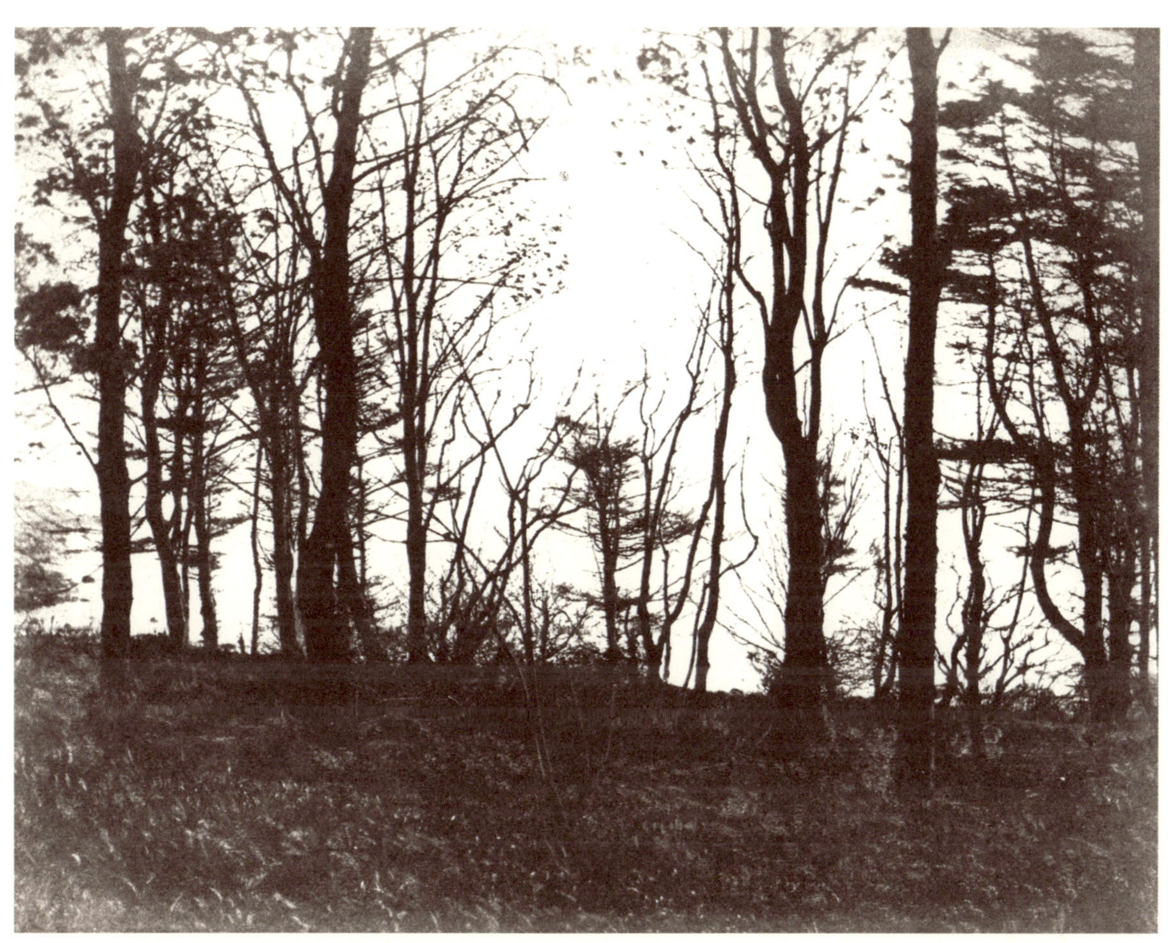

62 **Trees on the skyline**
salt paper print from a calotype negative
120 × 152 mm
PGP-W93

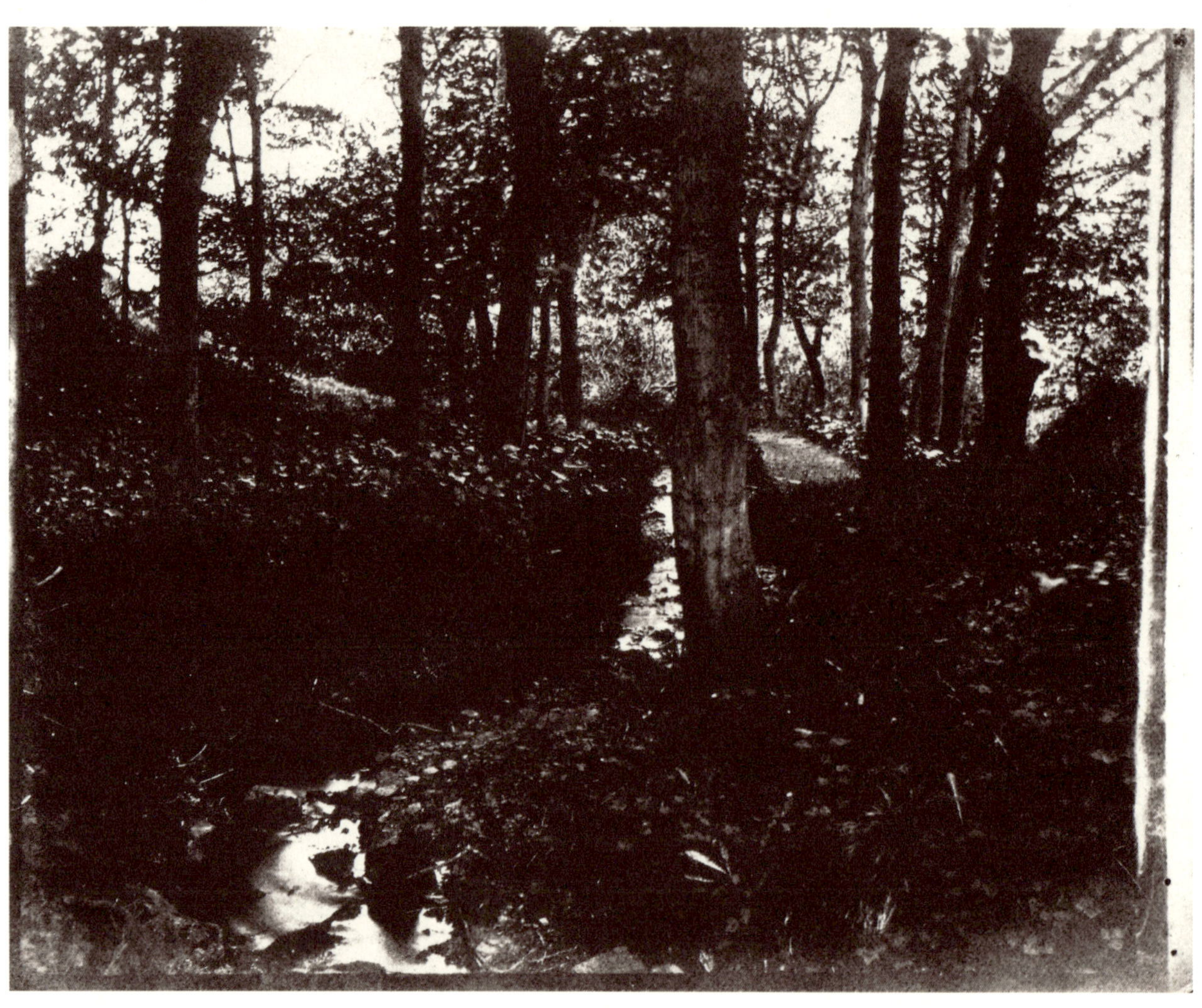

63 **A woodland stream**
salt paper print from a calotype negative
130 × 160 mm
PGP-W97

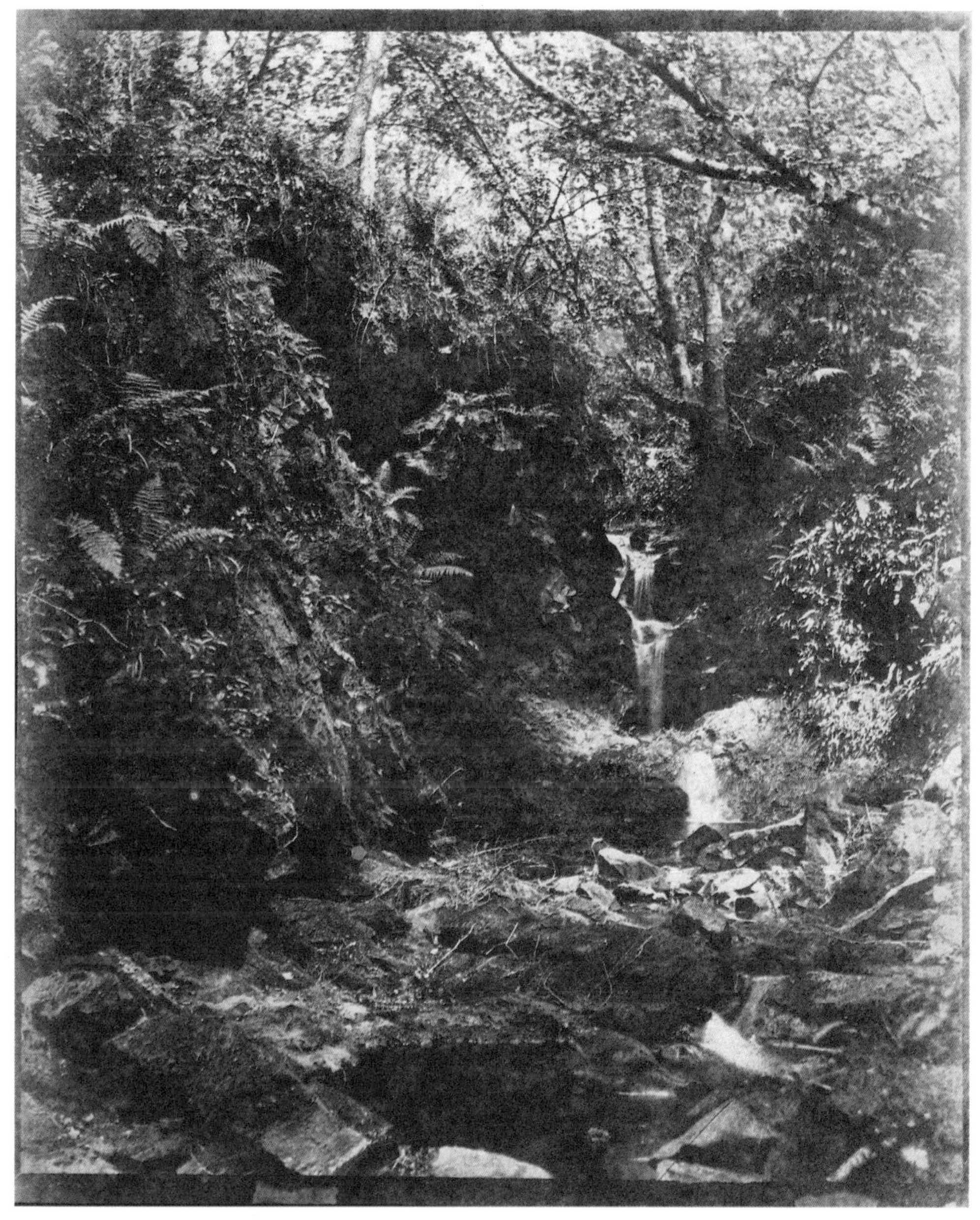

64 **Waterfall in a wood**
salt paper print from a calotype negative
161 × 129 mm
PGP-W101

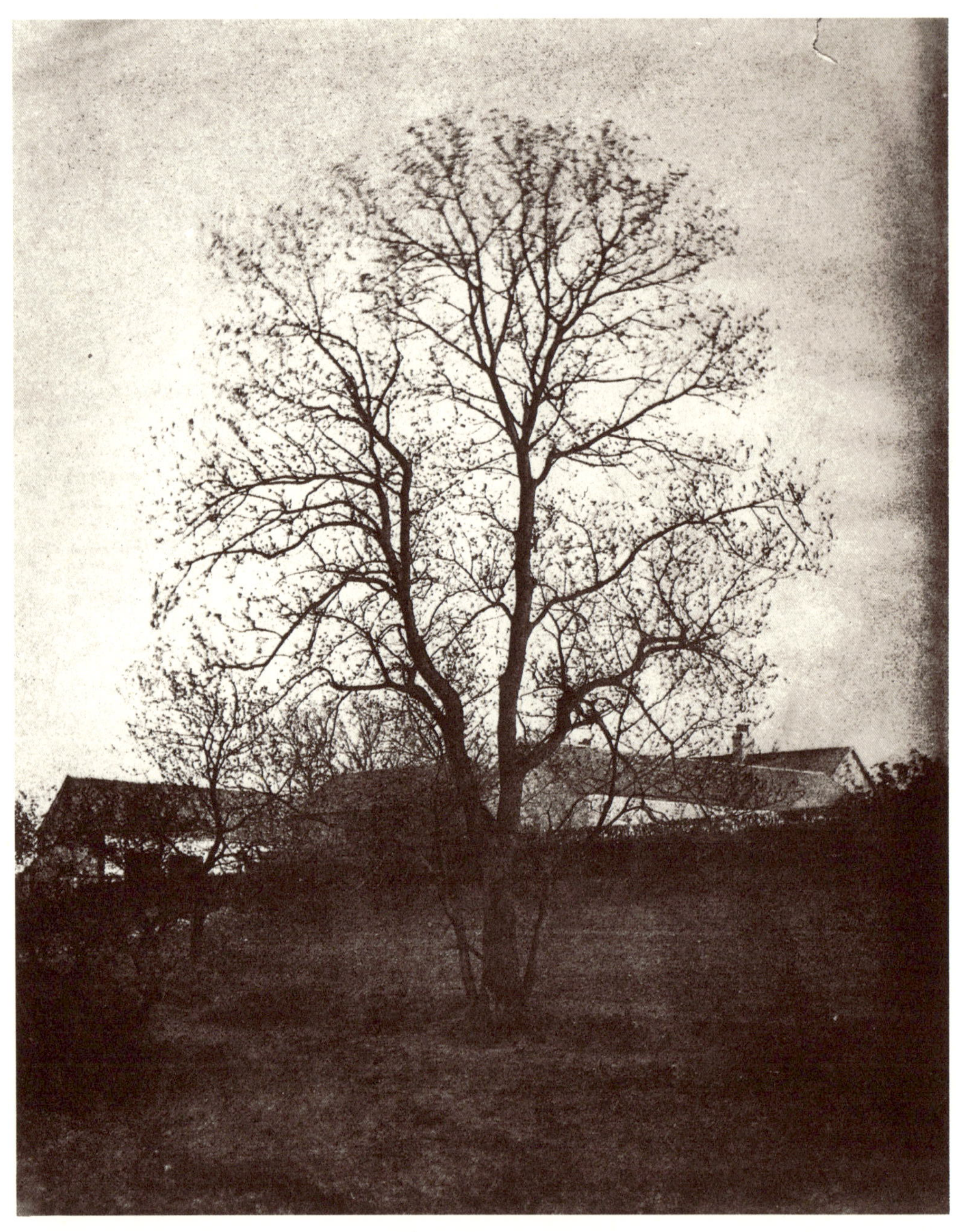

65 **Tree study**
albumenised salt print from a calotype negative
overhanging branch touched out in the negative
paper, 'J WHATMAN 1841'
240 × 196 mm
PGP-W106

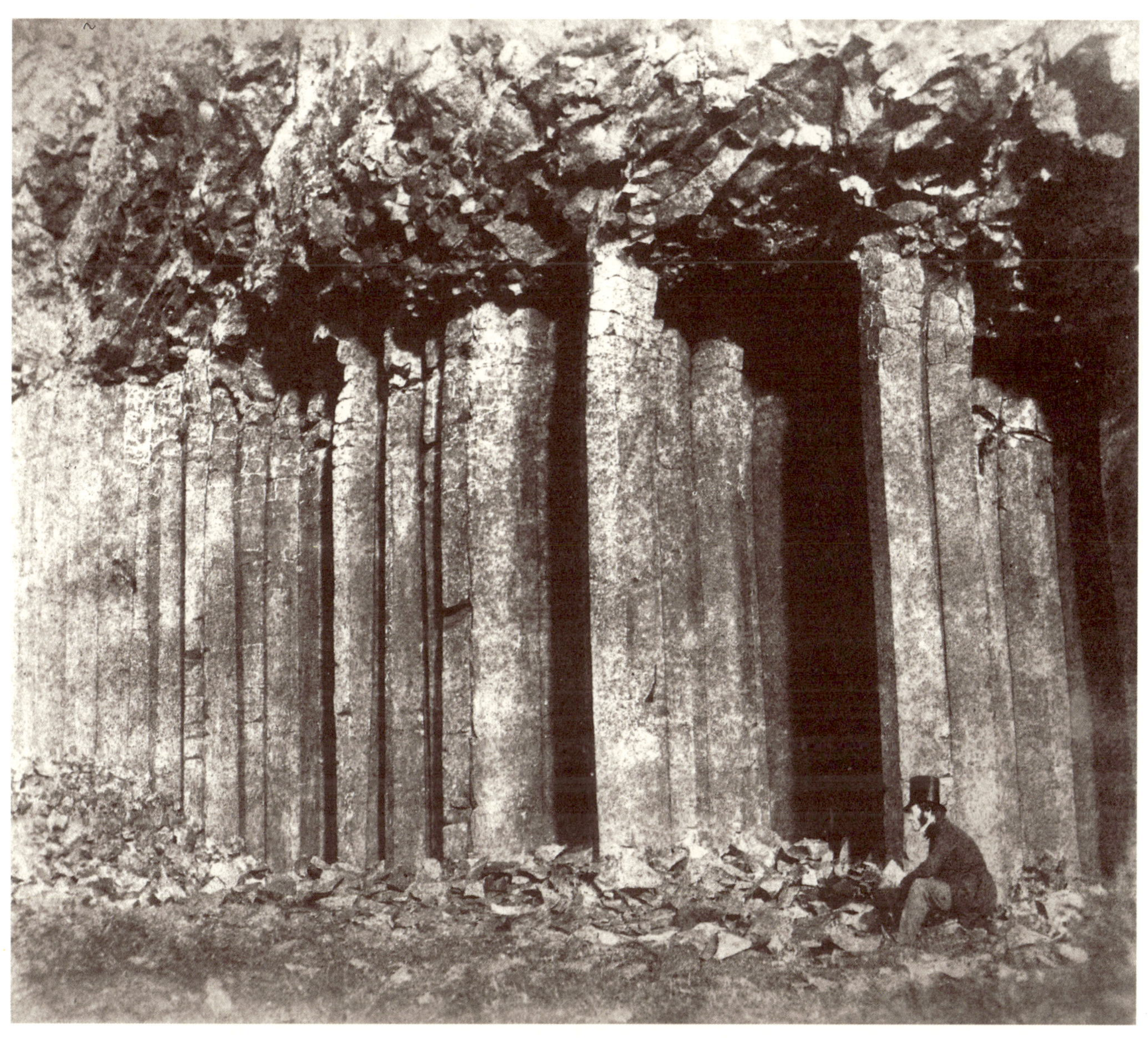

66 **Staffa, near Fingal's Cave**
the seated figure may be John Muir Wood
salt paper print from a calotype negative
paper, 'J WHATMAN TURKEY MILL'
170 × 192 mm
PGP-W70